Toxic Parents: How 5 Daughters Recover from the Emotional Abuse of Narcissistic Parents

By: Marissa Horn, Carly Sunjay, Faye Nasseri, Jennifer Day Goodson, Sarah Glenn

I0425582

Copyright / Publisher's Disclaimer:

Introduction

If you are reading this book, it is likely for a reason. You are looking to see if ANYONE else has had (or is having) the same kind of crappy and toxic "parenting" that your own parents have put you through, right? ...and you want some hope and encouragement that life isn't always going to be as hard as it is now?

Toxic Parents: How 5 Daughters Recover from the Emotional Abuse of Narcissistic Parents is the culmination of 5 stories of 5 brave women who have had to deal with the trauma of a toxic mother, father, or both. These are women who have come from all walks of life, financial backgrounds, sexual orientations and in some cases, even different countries. You will read about stolen childhoods, stolen innocence, physical and mental abuse, alcohol and drug abuse. You will read about how several of these authors even had thoughts and attempts of suicide and self-harming episodes.

But you know what? They all made it through! They made it past the traumatic childhood and later found (at least) reasonable happiness, joy and/or contentment once they left the hell's gates of their parents' households. And they want you to know that you can find happiness too! It's not easy even once you leave, as you have to discover your true self and what gives you unhinged happiness first, but they give you their road maps of how they re-gathered their lives and eventually made them worth living. They also give you their advice on your ongoing relationship with your parents – OR whether you should even HAVE an ongoing relationship with them. They all have differing opinions based on their similar yet differing experiences.

But one thing is for certain – you are not alone on your journey to healing. There are people just like you trying to put the shattered pieces of their lives together. And these five survivors want not only to share their stories with you, but also share their discoveries for healing so that you can have that hope as well.

Don't forget, though, that seeing a professional to help you work through your trauma is always a fantastic idea and we recommend it whole-heartedly. And if you do seek out a professional therapist, make sure you find one that you connect with. Therapists, fortunately or unfortunately, don't come in a "one-size-fits-all"; they all have different personalities and techniques. Like any relationship, don't settle if it doesn't feel right. If you don't feel a connection with the first therapist, try a second and third or however many it takes until you find a therapist whom you feel you can "spill your guts to" and feel great about it at the end of a session. This should be a person whom you look forward to seeing and talking to on an ongoing basis - not dreading it.

Chapter 1a: Marissa's Toxic Parents Story – The Beginnings

I remember one of the first days I got there [to my father's house] I had to share a bed with him and I just kept repeating this in my head: "Please don't rape me. Please don't rape me."

My father lived a fairly average life until my grandfather shot and killed himself when my dad was 16. My grandad had cheated on my grandmother, divorced her, and engaged the mistress, but I think he couldn't handle the guilt of it all. My dad then went from boarding school to boarding school, always getting kicked out for bad behavior. My dad actually had a toxic mother. I think he may have picked up these traits from her and that's why he turned out to be a toxic parent himself.

My dad took a lot of acid in his early days, and I think it messed with his head a bit. Maybe a bad trip that screwed him for life. That can actually happen. Or maybe it was the time that he was essentially dead after hanging himself after taking acid, he was already blue in the face when my mom found him. She resuscitated him herself until the ambulance came. It could have been that factor.

I was born in 1999 when my mother was only 19. She was actually never supposed to be able to have children due to fertility problems, but I happened anyway. She was still a kid and was never ready for it. She had a troubled upbringing. Her mother left her when she was young, and she never saw her again, so with her dad being a single parent she had to help raise her brother and sister. She didn't have a chance at having a childhood. I think that is why she still hasn't grown up.

When she was 14, she got into a car accident, and it fucked her up physically and mentally. The doctors didn't give her strong enough pain medication, and so she turned to stealing medication from her friend's parents medicine cabinets, then soon after she started drinking heavily, got into the wrong crowd and ran away from home. She took her sister's jacket with her. She found herself in a brothel and was selling her body for money to survive, and then one day her dad knocked on the door.

"Your sister wants her jacket back," is all he said to her.

Her entire life was filled with disappointment and sadness. She definitely wasn't ready to have me at the ripe age of 19. And my father definitely wasn't ready either. Even though he was 29, I don't think he ever was or ever will be. Some people just shouldn't have children. After I was born, my mom only realized who my father really was. He started drinking, and she got to see the real man behind the façade. I'm pretty sure I would never have been born if she got away from him earlier.

She noticed his incessant drinking. On some nights my dad would drink an entire bottle of whiskey in one night. He told me he did it because it helps him sleep. That is not true. He is just an alcoholic. An emotionally and physically abusive alcoholic. She once explained it to me, and it made total sense: when he drinks, he reverts back to a caveman. His thoughts, his actions, everything is uncivilized, and he just becomes a whole different person.

For this reason, she tried to keep me away from him except for occasional visits when he asked. I know it felt terrible for him, but he didn't deserve to see me. I would have been so much better off without my father in my life. There are so many lasting scars because of him. And I'm not sure if I could ever change that.

Although my mother has her flaws, one thing I can attribute to her is that she gave me the best childhood I could have asked for. Although I don't remember much of it, what I do remember is all pleasant, and I didn't even know about the alcohol and drug abuse.

My mom was going through financial trouble even though she worked two jobs at the time, and my father refused to give her any child support.

"The only way I'm going to help is if she stays with me," he said over the phone when she asked him for help. I understand now that he was fully in his rights to do this since they hadn't gotten married and signed any contracts that legally bound him to pay child support when they split apart.

So that's how I ended up traveling for a day to go live with my father for the first time, ever. I remember one of the first days I got there I had to share a bed with him and I just kept repeating this in my head: "Please don't rape me. Please don't rape me."

I'm not even sure how I would think of something like that at such a young age, and it still irks me to this day. How did I come up with that? Why?

If this was a movie, it would sort of be a foreshadowing of what was to come.

Chapter 1b: Getting to know the real him

Then I woke up. My own father was in my bed with me. Touching me. And he was too drunk to even understand what he was doing.

I didn't see my mother for years while I was staying with my father. My dad contradicted himself often. He'd say one thing and do the complete opposite. He'd often say, "Your mother abandoned you," and I'd believe him because I was young and impressionable. On the other hand, both of my parents would say they'd never bad mouth each other because they needed to set a good example for their child.

For the longest time, I believed what he said, and I think this was the start of all my mental health problems. My mother was always a sore subject for me because I missed her so much, she was back in a completely different state than I was, 1000s of miles away. All the other kids in my school had stable families, their mother and father were still together, and everyone was happy. But I had a very cynical view of it, and I loathed people for having happy lives. It was really unhealthy to have those views at such a young age, but I was conditioned to it.

There was never any stability, I had to look after my father all the time and had to grow up fast. I had to cook, clean, and still study and do homework as well because my father wouldn't lift a finger, even just for himself. My dad is still like that to this day, he expects everything to be done for him without regard to other people. Since then I've been just living in constant tiredness. It is physical, but also emotional, I *feel* tired. I've never been able to shake that feeling, and I do hope no other people will have to feel this way. I've just always had to do everything for everyone around me when I was meant to be having a childhood, learning and growing.

In grade 4 (at age 11) my dad drank an entire bottle of whiskey before bed. It marked one of the most traumatic and life-altering things to ever have happened to me. I feel like I may have predicted it that night and for the longest time, I blamed myself for not preventing it from happening.

I remember getting a bottle of pepper spray my mother gave me before I left home and I kept it next to my bed. I was tired and ended up going to sleep anyway. I dreamt about a girl from my school exposing herself in front of everyone, and I felt terrible about it, so I tried to stop her from doing it so as to prevent any further embarrassment.

Then I woke up. My own father was in my bed with me. Touching me. And he was too drunk to even understand what he was doing. At least that was his excuse for years. I jumped out of bed and made my way to the kitchen, and had a complete breakdown at 11. I cried for I don't know how long. It felt like 2 minutes but at the same time 2 hours. One thing I will never forget is how I grabbed a knife out of the drawer and contemplated killing my father. He was back in his room. I was so young, yet I completely understood what had happened to me.

And what did I do? Nothing. I put the knife back into the drawer. That was the day that I lost a piece of myself. It buried itself so deep inside the depths of my mind that I never got it back.

He heard me crying and called me over. He didn't understand why I was crying. He didn't know what he had done.

"You should eat," he said, looking concerned. He really didn't know what he did. I continued crying and didn't say anything. I finally calmed down, and we went to sleep in the same bed. He insisted. But I think he was genuinely concerned because he didn't know why on earth I was crying. I was scared it would happen again and wrapped myself so tightly into the tiniest ball of a human being you could imagine that I, in my own eyes, virtually disappeared, which was all I wanted at that point in time.

So, I did what I thought was right and went to school the next day, and tried my best to pretend that nothing happened the night before. It was the first time in my life that I decided to cover up such intense, harmful emotions and I was never taught how I should deal with something like this. Do I tell a teacher and they call the police, and he gets arrested, and I don't have a home anymore? Do I tell a friend and keep it a secret, even though they would end up telling an adult out of concern for my safety? My answer to all of those questions was to say no, it's too much of a hassle. It will complicate things.

"Just bury it deep inside and forget about it," I'd often tell myself when I wanted to speak out. One day a teacher came up to me when I burst out crying in recess. She kept asking me what was wrong, and I lied, "I got kicked off the soccer team because I'm a girl," and she left me alone after that. No questions asked. And that was the closest I ever got to telling anyone anything about it for 4 months.

I'd keep a box that I used to put my toys in wedged between my bedroom door and closet so that my dad couldn't enter my room at night. I lived in fear of letting that happen to myself again.

Why didn't you protect yourself? Why didn't you do better? Why didn't you lock your door?

I started seeing my mother again after not seeing her for about 6 months. She moved to my state so that she could be closer to me. She babysat me that night while my dad was out with a friend or a lover. I don't know. It took me an entire quarter of the movie to muster up the courage to tell her what happened. When I finally did, she understandably freaked out. We left my dad's house swiftly and went to her apartment.

We cried together, and I know she also blamed herself for what happened. She had similar things happen to her when she was a kid, and her sexual relationship with my father was rocky, to say the least.

We tried to report it to the police. There was no evidence. So, they didn't believe me. A social worker told my mom, when I was right in front of her, "Well, I don't know. Kids lie about these things sometimes." What was I supposed to do, film my innocence being lost? How do they think these types of cases even work?

This broke me. The justice system failed me. They wouldn't let me be heard. So, I became smaller, and smaller, losing more parts of myself that I'll never get back, like puzzle pieces. Once you lose one piece of a puzzle, it will never be complete again, and at some point, it'll become unrecognizable. Is it even a puzzle any more if there are no pieces to put together?

Years after the incident with my dad, he tried to make excuses: "I didn't know what I was doing. I don't even remember. I was sleepwalking. I have a sleep disorder."

I never fell for those excuses. It is honestly inexcusable. I also found out that my dad had molested my cousin, and he got caught by my uncle, who didn't do anything and just let it slide. I blamed myself for what happened to her. I wasn't staying with my dad at the time, I was with my mother. She took me out of the hospital at 3 o clock in the morning after I had my stomach pumped from trying to overdose on medication. I was in grade 8 at the time and couldn't handle the pressures of school and home life. It is definitely something that I regret, but the doctor said he was surprised that I was still alive when he saw me. Since that day, I became grateful for still being here. Since I survived, it had to be for a reason, right?

Another major factor in our dysfunctional relationship was the invasion of privacy. He would look through all my stuff. Ask questions about everything. All the people I was talking to, and for example, if he wanted to go through my phone and I denied it, he would freak out and ask me what I was hiding. I was never allowed any personal space, and he would always be around me, hovering, not giving me any freedom. He would shout at me about this a lot. I don't take kindly to shouting, I can't handle it. It just makes me cry.

Chapter 1c: Nothing Makes Any Sense

If something isn't perfect in the eyes of a toxic parent, it's like it's the end of the world for them. Remember at the end of the day, that not everything needs to be perfect.

I would live in fear almost every night. Just wanting help, just hoping someone would come to save me. I was scared of my dad. Sometimes he would get so drunk that he'd talk to an imaginary person in the room with him. It was honestly terrifying for me to see that as a kid. I would often lock my door in fear of him coming into my room at night. He'd do that when he got drunk, and stand in the doorway and hover there, and try to talk to me. Note that I was a child, in primary school, being woken up by a person that was so blackout drunk that he'd often piss his own bed.

"FUCK YOU, YOU STUPID FUCKING BITCH," he shouted after he knocked on my door for two hours straight because I had it locked. I slept with a knife under my pillow that night, just in case I needed it to protect myself. He was so drunk that he screamed at me. What was so important that he needed to be in my room at that time of night? I feared for my life.

It was around that time that I had my first experience of suicidal thoughts due to being treated this way. I couldn't do anything about it. He would do these things, but because he was so drunk, the next day, he would remember nothing of it, and I just kept silent about it. I never stood up for myself, and I never had a voice for the longest time.

Growing up didn't happen as gradually, and healthily as it should have, but instead, it happened abruptly. I had to be conscious of every single action, every single word I said in fear of somehow upsetting my father. A simple, innocent action or word could set my father off into a spiral which would result in me crying, mostly out of frustration of not being listened to, and him shouting.

It's actually difficult to explain what it was like having an argument with him. He would "project" a lot, which is a defense mechanism he used in order to remain in denial of his own problems. If he felt or did something, that he didn't like himself, he'd project them onto me and shift the blame. He would also interpret things in utterly ridiculous ways and try and change the reality of things by way of misinterpretation/looking for a deeper meaning in something that isn't there.

For example, if I ever dared to make coffee for myself when I got home from school and not for him, he would actually get upset with me. Coffee was actually the cause of many of our fights, and it's absolutely ridiculous. The reason for that is because I'd try and sit him down and explain to him, calmly and logically, that it really isn't a problem, it's not that deep. But he'd just turn it into something bigger than it actually was. My biggest issue was that I cooked, cleaned, and made multiple cups of coffee for him for many years in a row, and I still had schoolwork and studying to do. I was exhausted.

The usual guilt-tripping would be thrown in on his part during an argument. "But it's not about you not making me coffee, it's about how I would make you coffee every time I made some for myself, and it's disrespectful for you to do this to me. If I made enough money, I'd put all my money into a bowl, and everyone in the household could take what they need and give back if they want to," he'd go on rants like these for hours at a time.

I am still scared of him when he drinks to this day because he always overdoes it. I have seen him stumbling everywhere and so drunk he'd forget what he was saying two seconds after saying it. I've spent hours convincing him to go to bed because he never knew when to stop. Otherwise, he would make a fool of himself.

He would take me out drinking with him before I reached the legal drinking age, and I had lost count the number of times he drove me home when he was drunk. He's gotten so drunk that he tried to start a fight with my boyfriends' best friend for no reason. He would flirt with already taken women, make inappropriate jokes about rape, children, and overall just make me uncomfortable. Hell, my dad tried to take me out of high school and get me to start my own business that wouldn't have gone anywhere or benefitted anything, just because my grades weren't as good as he wanted them to be. If something isn't perfect in the eyes of a toxic parent, it's like it's the end of the world for them. Remember at the end of the day, that not everything needs to be perfect.

My dad is a very broken person, and I don't think anyone should have let him raise a child. The only positive thing I learned from him was what not to do. I learned from his mistakes. At 17, he told me that the only way to help yourself if you are having problems is to drink till you black out and you forget about it for a while.

I obviously never listened to him when he suggested it. I don't want to be like him, I never want to become my father. My fear is making the same mistakes my parents made. So I don't drink. I don't do drugs, because what if I become like them if I was under the influence? What if I acted just like them and broke my own promise to myself?

My dad has lost two jobs due to his drinking, the first time it happened, he went on a one-month drinking binge and eventually got fired for not coming into the office anymore. I was living with him during both those times. As you could imagine, there was a lot of fighting during that time. When he lost the first job, he sat around all day playing a video game for 12-24 hours almost every day and didn't do anything. I had no work experience, so I ended up getting a low paying job to help with some of the funds. I ended up having to sell the second-hand car my dad gave me before I graduated so that I could pay the rent.

 He finally got a job after many hour-long conversations of me trying to convince him to do *something* and not sit around all day. Things were stable for a while until he got too drunk at a work function and said some inappropriate things and got himself fired again. Another couple of months of no work for him again. So, I saved my money and moved into my own apartment with my boyfriend because I couldn't deal with that environment anymore. It was just so emotionally exhausting.

Chapter 1d: Working Through It

a. Gaslighting and DID

We were sitting in a coffee shop. I hadn't seen my mom for weeks, months even, and without any word from her at all. She did that. Often.

"Yeah, so ever since you were young, I noticed something really weird about you. You'd be yourself, the next minute not." Mom said. "Whoever that personality is, I know that she doesn't like me, she hates me. I can see it on your face, you become very rude and have very little respect for me. It's been happening since you were very young. Have you ever heard of DID?"

"Yeah?" I said, and my heart sank in my chest.

Mom proceeded to pull up a webpage explaining what dissociative identity disorder is. Obviously, I know what that is. It's the fancy name for multiple personality disorder.

What the fuck is she going on about?

I think she was literally referring to the stage in my life when my hormones were all out of whack, I was starting to get moody, and trying to figure out what was happening to me. Everyone goes through that. But other than that, I think she was referring to the period when I stayed with her, and her drug abuse got very excessive, where she would be offended over a simple conversation, twist my words to make it look like I was trying to fight with her. It made me feel like I was crazy. I didn't even want to say anything to her at one point out of fear of somehow saying something wrong and her getting offended.

After everything we'd been through, she was trying to come up with a "logical" explanation for all the shit that happened. My mom disappears a lot, she packs up her shit at the slightest sign of trouble, never facing the issues but rather running away from them. She could never accept responsibility for her actions. This was in the same boat though, she would much rather shift blame for her wrongdoings onto me, a 16-year-old girl, rather than face her true self and her own problems.

When I got home that day, I just cried. For hours. I honestly believed her. She actually made me think I had a mental illness that I didn't have. I believed it for days, even weeks.

Later in life, I learned that this was a form of gaslighting. This is something an abuser will do to manipulate you into questioning your own sanity for their own benefit. Fucked up, right?

My mom and I were living alone together when I was 15 after she'd broken up with her previous boyfriend, who was an absolute nutcase. He threatened to shoot her when she tried to leave him, he also took all the money she earned from her job; he was a real pothead. He would smoke a joint before work, come home during a lunch break from work and smoke another joint, then have a couple of joints at night before bed. It got nasty at some point because it was affecting the financial situation of our household.

Everything was actually perfect for a while after that. She had a stable job, I did well in school, but everything deteriorated when she couldn't handle the pressure anymore. She tried to overdose on pills and booked herself into a mental health institution. She was gone for 2 months and when she got back to work, her job didn't pay her and they dismissed her unfairly, so we had to pay the rent late. The landlord wouldn't stand for that though and told us that we need to be out of the apartment the next day.

We moved into her friend Matt's apartment and lived with him for a while. She was trying to find new work, but nothing came up, although her friend promised that he would look after us. Her friend soon after got retrenched, so we had to figure something else out. My mother then spoke to me and said that she was thinking about going back to sex work. I was just a kid, so I didn't know what to say, but we were desperate for money.

"Yeah? Okay. Maybe that's a good idea," I said. Note that I am only a 15-year-old kid in this situation. Her drug use started getting bad. Every time I was around her, she was either high or coming down from the drugs.

Dealing with someone like that when you're only a kid is difficult, to say the least. She could never hold a conversation, would never listen, and continuously misunderstood what you were trying to say. She would often interpret the things in a way that made it look like the whole world was against her, which in my opinion, is incredibly self-destructive behavior.

This is what I think made her believe that I had multiple personality disorder and that one of my personalities hated her. She needed something to justify what went through her head. Years later I found out that she resented me for telling her to go into prostitution again, as if I forced her into it, another example of her not accepting responsibility for her own actions. She said that it hurt her that I would even suggest something like that as if I was the one that made her do it. She is my mother, a grown, adult woman, that came up to me, a child, and told me she was thinking of going back into prostitution because we were broke and nearly homeless, what did she expect me to say?

Things were weird for a while when we were living with her friend. They were sort of dating. But she also had a sugar daddy. And another boyfriend. For some reason, she started getting jealous of Matt and me. She was so delusional that she literally thought I was having sex with a man the same age as my father. Then one day she went out and never came back. A few weeks went by, and I wasn't doing very okay mentally so I kept skipping school saying I was sick. My school ended up calling my father as they couldn't get a hold of my mother. She turns her phone off when she disappears like that.

My mother then tried to report her friend Matt to the police for kidnapping me, when she was the one that left me behind, which was really confusing to me. I ended up moving back in with my dad. From one bad situation to the next.

She told me years later that the situation we were in was my fault and that I shouldn't have made her get into prostitution. My mother would blame literally everyone else but herself for events that she created.

b. Anti-social and dismissive of your feelings and opinions

It was only between the age of 16/17 that I learned how to stand up for myself. Before that, I would just nod along and say, "Okay. Yeah. Cool," instead of giving my opinion and letting myself be heard. I am 19 now and only now learning how to stand up for myself properly, due to encouragement from a loved one.

My dad ingrained my antisocial behavior into me at a young age. I am still trying to work on it since I never really had friends, and I still don't. I tried to make friends with people, but I would never actually be able to hang out with them because my dad would make me feel bad for trying to ask him to drop me off at a friend's place. Or even say that he didn't trust me enough to let me go off on my own. I didn't smoke, drink, or do drugs, or party, all I wanted to do was have some friends to call my own, and I was denied that most of my teenage years. As a result, my basic social skills such as small talk with strangers seems nearly impossible to me.

I had to teach myself how to speak to people without getting nervous and wanting to go back home immediately because of my embarrassing lack of such a basic human skill.

"You just have to learn that you don't need people. You don't need friends, they will just disappoint you. Trying to have friends is such a waste of time," my dad said this to me once, and it stuck with me ever since. He was not a social person. In my entire adolescence I never once saw him hang out with one friend, except one woman that he saw for a couple months.

So I guess I lead by his example and now I have no friend to show for it except for family and mutual friends of my current partner. I have been trying though, I have been getting better. I can say hi to strangers now, I can hold a conversation with an acquaintance and most of the time handle hanging out with a few friends before burning out.

If you are or were in a similar situation, I would definitely suggest going out more. Go see the world and meet new people outside of your normal everyday routine. I'm not saying you need to travel the world and leave everything behind. Just take a step away and have people around you that will benefit your life, and whose lives you can benefit too. Learn how to speak about your feelings and allow yourself to have strong opinions.

Allow yourself to risk being in disagreement with someone, remember that it is not the end of the world and not everyone out there will berate and belittle you for your thoughts and feelings. Communication is a vital part of any relationship you have in life as it forms the foundation of what that relationship is built on. So, tell that person how you feel, and always remember that people are actually surprisingly understanding and considerate, not everything you say will be taken personally, as a toxic parent would do.

One of the biggest (recurring) arguments I ever had with my partner was my inability to communicate/my lack of communication. Whatever decision needed to be made, I would just agree with my partner or just let him decide, no matter what it was, or if it was a good idea or not. Or I would just say I liked something just because he did, and agree with everything he said.

In his eyes I'm sure it came off as very artificial and rather frustrating to deal with, my character no longer had the depth and complexity that he thought I had because I closed myself off from the world again. I really think this was out of fear of being judged, because for years before that I was taught that every opinion and thought I had was invalid. That everything I did was wrong, and I know it was illogical, but I was scared that I would feel those same feelings again. Of being rejected by someone I loved for simply being who I am.

I was scared that he would like me less because I enjoyed something he didn't like or vice versa. I now know that it was incredibly childish and I wish I weren't like that. I lost a bit of my personality because of never growing as a person, and I felt as if I hardly have any of me left anymore.

Just slowly work on it, slowly build yourself back up. Become a healthy, independent person that doesn't have to consider everyone's feelings in everything you do. Learn that it is okay to not always be right in what you say and do. Don't stress so much about making a mistake. It is part of life. Relax. You need to mess up to grow. You don't always have to agree with everyone, and neither does everyone have to agree with you.

You will just end up being your own worst enemy if you keep beating yourself up about every little thing and worrying about all the small, unimportant things. You just need to remember, that at the end of the day, you are the only person that will always be there for you, through thick and thin. You are the only person that you can really change for the better, and learn to appreciate that. Love and treat your body in the best possible way. You only have one body. Make the best of it.

c. Everything is going to be okay

"Everything is going to be okay," a phrase I heard very often.

I used to hate it when my mother said this to me when I was struggling. Years later I realized that it is true. I went through so much, I experienced so many things that a child shouldn't have to experience, but I did it. I soldiered on, and now I have a fantastic job, an apartment of my own, and a loving boyfriend to come home to. In my darkest times, I would never have believed that I would come so far, I'd call someone crazy if they told me that.

It is okay to cry. It is okay to break down your walls. It is okay to feel more than you can handle.

But you know what? Even in your darkest of times, you will always find a light. There will always be someone there for you, be it you or a friend or a family member. Appreciate the friends you have and open up to them about things for once. Talk to them. Actually, get to know them. You will be surprised how much simply getting all of that off your chest will help. In doing so, you will get to know yourself better as well. It is very easy to get lost inside your own head and forget who you are. Simply saying things out loud will help you conceptualize your thoughts and begin to understand them even more.

Just breathe. No matter how hard things are right now, or were back then, they are going to get better. It is impossible for nothing good to come of your life. Love yourself, and love your life. If things are bad, change them. If you don't like something about yourself, change it.

Remember that there is nothing shameful about going to therapy. It is worth it, and it will help you come to terms with everything and maybe unlearn some nasty habits that are a result of your toxic parents.

d. Self Esteem

Toxic parents belittle and degrade you often. This can put a real damper on your self-esteem. I never felt like anything I did was good enough, and as a result, this affected my life negatively. I didn't go out and do the things I wanted to do. I never pursued any hobbies or tried to work on any talents because I just thought: "I'll never be good at anything anyway." No matter what you say or do, a toxic parent will always think their way is the only way, and anything that doesn't fall in line with what they're feeling isn't the right way.

Trust yourself. Trust your emotions. Toxic parents will make you out to be crazy, like you shouldn't be feeling certain things, or you're feeling them wrong, you're not feeling them enough, or you're feeling them too strongly. This will put so much doubt inside of you, but I promise! You are not crazy. You are a human being with complex thoughts and feelings, and that is nothing to be ashamed of.

When I was suffering from severe depression and tried to talk to my dad about it to try and get help, my dad completely disregarded it and made my problems look so minuscule and worthless.

"I have had depression for years, and I'm still fine! You just need to suck it up and get over it," a classic case of my-problems-are-worse-so-yours-can't-be-so-bad. This discussion with him lasted about three hours, nothing was resolved, and I just left crying because the conversation just went in circles and none of it made sense at all. I felt like I was crazy.

You owe your toxic parents nothing. You don't need to prove your worth to them. You don't need to prove that your feelings are valid. You don't need to help them after they have subjected you to years of abuse. Instead, put your energy towards bettering your own life and becoming healthy and happy again.

I bit the bullet and decided to pursue something I am passionate about and turned it into a career too. Along the way, I always doubted myself and almost gave up too many times to count, but I wanted to prove to myself, that I could do it, I could make it.

In times like these, remind yourself, that nothing good will come if you never try. Anything good in life happens with hard work. Reach for your dreams. If it doesn't work out, just try again! Move on to the next thing if it really isn't meant to be. Life is all about trial and error.

e. Healing

Learn how to set boundaries. If you are an adult or almost an adult, you are fully capable of making your own choices in life. If you are with your parents and notice that their toxic behavior is affecting your enjoyment at say some event that you are both attending, it's ok to stay away from them or leave early. You don't have to subject yourself to more abuse just because you feel you need to be polite, or you want to make your parents happy. You also don't need to hang out with them just because you feel obligated to, you can just say no. As toxic parents they will likely try to make you feel guilty about it, but let it roll off your back. It's time for you to become your own person and not have your emotions manipulated by someone else. Your happiness is up to you, and if you let your toxic parents (or anyone else) control how you feel, you will never achieve true happiness.

That is actually true of your parents, as well. They (not you) are responsible for their own happiness (or unhappiness). It is not your responsibility to make them happy by putting up with their abusive behavior just because they make you feel like you have to. If at any moment they are name-calling, criticizing the right choices you make in life, or just making a fool of you or themselves, call it quits. They may take it personally but know that this is best for YOU and your mental health. They have controlled you all these years by exploiting the guilt that they make you feel to get their way, and it is your choice to stop that from happening again.

If you currently live apart from your parents and decide to stay distanced from them because you know the toxic behavior will never end, that is okay. Remember that you are supposed to look after yourself, your well-being, and they no longer have control over you. You may feel like you owe them everything due to the societal standards that are set up regarding your responsibilities to family and your parents. Or it could be that they conditioned you into thinking that you owe them everything.

But if you have toxic parents or toxic family members, you owe them nothing.

You don't have to be at your parents' beck and call every hour of the day. For example, my dad has been going through another period of unemployment, and he asked me to take him to interviews, lend him money, and just in general run errands for him. I didn't have to do them, but I did because I felt bad for him even though I have my own responsibilities to deal with. I felt like it was my responsibility to help him. It may sound bitter, but why would I owe him anything after everything he's put me through? He was just taking advantage of the kind nature that he knows I have. It's all about what you can do for *them* and what benefits their agenda, no matter your circumstances.

Learn to identify these things and learn how to say no. Learn that their problem is not your problem. They are grown adults, and they should learn that having a child does not mean they are a slave that must do everything for them at a snap of their fingers. So, stand up for yourself and make it clear why it isn't okay.

Stop trying to please them. A common trait of a toxic parent is that they are overly critical in everything you do or say. If you were brought up in a toxic environment, you do not owe them the time of day. You don't have to worry about gaining their approval of everything. They will likely not give it to you, anyway, and somehow find an issue with whatever decisions you make so that they have something to complain about. Toxic parents will never be happy with anything you do, especially something that they don't have control over. They want to dictate every step you make in life, and if it isn't their way, it's the wrong way. Don't buy into it!

Toxic parents will not look further than their own opinions and regard anything other than what they think, as incorrect or offensive. They are stubborn and will never change their minds. I have spent hours trying to convince my father to listen to me, and understand what I am trying to say. But they don't listen, they speak so they can respond and cause an issue rather than listen and understand someone else's point of view. That is why you feel as though you are never heard or understood by them. Remember, not everyone is like that. In fact, most aren't. Don't let your parents skew your outlook on other people. Don't let them set the bar for what to expect other people to be like.

You will meet people that treat you well, you will meet people that will improve your life, and you will be happy. Be patient and be kind to yourself. Healing is a long and arduous task but will be worth it in the end. I promise that if you try hard enough, you will get out of the unhealthy cycle your parent/s forced you into. In time you will learn to accept your imperfections. Everyone has them!

You cannot change how your parents are, and they will not improve themselves. A part of being a toxic parent comes with not taking responsibility for themselves and not realizing what they do. Because of this, they will not change. They refuse to acknowledge that what they do is wrong or that they need to change their behavior. You need to accept that there is nothing you can do about that, and adapt your life to it accordingly, even if it means disassociating yourself from your parents completely. You can control how you react to them, how you treat them, and to what extent they'll be a part of your life. Working on taking back control of your life won't be easy, but remember, everything is going to be okay.

f. Relationship now

My relationships with my mother and father have improved over the years. We have worked things out, but I don't include them in my life as much as most people do, out of fear of any of that toxicity becoming part of my life again. I distance myself slightly and only visit occasionally so we can have lunch and catch up. I don't give away too many details about my life to give either of my parents the opportunity to condemn my decisions.

My mother finally has a job again after two years of unemployment, and she has become more stable. Her drug use isn't consuming her life anymore, because every time she had a job, she would go on a drug binge and end up losing her job. She is herself again, and I can have a conversation with her without being interrupted constantly.

Our relationship was rocky throughout my entire adolescent years. We fought a lot. There was a period in time when she would lie about being under the influence of drugs. I obviously saw the signs of her being high because I experienced it so many times before. She would talk fast, not listen to what I would say, and would basically end up having a conversation with herself. She couldn't sit still, and you could see her mouth was dry when she spoke. It honestly always made me feel uncomfortable to be around her when she was like that and I would mostly just get angry at her and want to go home instead of being around that.

My boyfriend encouraged me to confront my mom about the situation when she lied to me about what she was doing. It's like she thought I was stupid, and got offended when I asked her if she was using drugs. When she was guilty of something, she'd become defensive and try shift blame by saying I was "disrespecting" her and she "doesn't appreciate being treated like this."

But in reality, I was merely concerned about her well-being, I couldn't help but be worried since every time I saw her, she was high. I even thought it was my fault at some point. She didn't even bother to keep off the drugs for a few hours to spend time with me. For years, she chose drugs over me. It felt like she loved the drugs more than she loved me. In my late teens, I even started using the same drugs she was using to try and see what all the fuss was about. Honestly, I would say that it's highly disappointing, looking at it now from a different perspective. All it does is keep you awake and spend three hours trying to sort your Tupperware in descending order according to size. Don't do drugs, kids.

I could feel myself slipping, I could feel myself slowly becoming like her, and you know what I did? Used more and more and more because I felt so terrible about what I was doing. Why would I do this? I'll just disappoint everyone around me, even myself, if I fall into the same trap as she did. I started drinking. I started having sex with men older than me. I went to school and wrote an exam while high. At least I passed it though. It was just a toxic cycle of doing precisely what my parents did to escape, so I started hating myself. I started hating the world around me.

And I understood. I fully realized why both of my parents abused substances. Everyone has their own way of getting rid of, or rather, masking the pain.

Sad? Take drugs. You'll feel okay for a while. Stressed, can't sleep? Drink until you black out. You won't feel anything until you wake up. But that's the thing. It is only temporary. You get that little bit of relief, for a few seconds or however long, but soon you'll come down, soon you'll wake up sober, and everything will come rushing straight back to you. I understand why my dad always drank so excessively, and never a few drinks just to chill out. If you drink a little bit and start getting to the drunk phase, you usually start feeling sad if you're going through a rough time in your sober life. So what he'd do, is drink a large amount, in a short amount of time, so he could black out and not have to deal with whatever feelings he was having. I think he liked that, so he kept doing it, over and over again, so that he didn't have to face any of his problems.

My dad, as a form of punishment, knowing that it upset me when he drank, would deliberately drive me to the store, and buy a bottle of expensive whiskey, and drink the entire thing the same day. A few months before I tried to kill myself in grade 8, he did precisely that.

I was self-harming at the time. It is an incredibly insufferable way to live your life. I would think about it every second of the day. Ways to do it during a bathroom break at school. I'd do it the night before Christmas, disregarding the fact that Christmas is meant to be the season of being jolly.

My dad would hear I was awake that night, and once it hit midnight, he called me over and showed me the present he got me, fully unaware of the fact that I just cried my eyes out for two hours and my body was stinging from hurting myself just a few minutes before. I know I was meant to be excited, I was meant to be happy, but I couldn't find a single thing to be happy about. My dad would shout at me often, he would drink almost every night, and as he did years before, knock on my door for hours.

I could say that this was by far the darkest time of my life. I tried to speak to my dad about it, and it's like he didn't take it seriously. When he found out that I self-harmed he just said, in a mocking tone: "So you really think you want to die?", And proceeded to push me down to the floor and choke me. He was trying to prove a point maybe, trying to somehow teach me that I didn't really want to die, or I was too much of a coward to go through with it. Maybe my problems weren't as severe as I thought they were, maybe if someone actually tried to kill me I would completely change and realize I was just a stupid teenager. Immediately after that, he thought it would be applicable to punish me by making me watch him drink an entire bottle of whiskey.

He went through my phone. He didn't let me have privacy, he would come into my room unannounced at any time of the day, stand behind me and hover over me while I did things on my computer. It completely broke the trust I had in him. So I stopped trying to talk to him, my self-harming got worse, I got better at hiding things to avoid facing any conflict. I became less and less myself as the days went by.

Then one day I just had enough. School was too much. I had too much homework, I couldn't handle the stresses at home, so one morning before school I took about 100 pills that I found in a spare room with me to school. The memories of that time of my life are kind of shady, so I don't really remember and understand what I could have been thinking that day. It was selfish of me to be doing it there, with all those people around. I didn't think about how it would affect other people. I just thought about how I needed to die.

My choice was utterly irrational. The last thing I remember about that day was dropping something in class, standing up from my desk to pick it up, and then it was all a blur. Apparently, at that point I fell over, someone caught me, and I was taken to the school office. They found evidence of what I did when they went through my stuff and called an ambulance. The next thing I remember is waking up in the hospital. They pumped my stomach. I took a concoction of blood pressure medication and pills my late aunt used to use for her schizophrenia. It is a miracle that I survived, and I am not much of a religious person.

There was a doctor sitting on a stool near me, and close family surrounded me. My dad, my grandmother, and my aunt and uncle were standing around me. I think they were all disappointed. Some of the friends that I knew for about three months visited too. They brought me gifts. They were the only people there that made me feel a slight glimmer of happiness. Seeing my family just made me feel ashamed of myself, and I felt terrible for what I had done.

When I was alone, my uncle spoke to me for a bit. "Do you know how much you hurt your aunt by doing this? You are so selfish. Why didn't you speak to her about this? You know she loves you."

He said this to me, and my heart broke. I kept a straight face and didn't say a thing. I don't remember the ride in the ambulance. My dad dropped everything the day I tried to kill myself and came straight to my school because he was so worried about me. I heard this from a friend I made at the school I attended when I explained my abusive situation at home. I even spoke to her about the sexual abuse I endured years prior. It's like she didn't care.

"But he rushed to the school when he heard what happened. He obviously cares about you," she said. When I told her about the sexual abuse, she said, "But I don't believe you. Are you sure that actually happened? He seems like such a nice guy."

Everyone left me at the hospital because I still needed treatment and nighttime fell. I had been in the intensive care unit for 3 days, unconscious. The school uniform I wore the day it happened was in a little cabinet next to my hospital bed. I was in a ward with 4 other people in it. There was a woman next to me with the same name as me. She was there due to a kidney stone.

I got my old school shirt from the cabinet and reached for a blade I had left in the pocket. It was the first thing I thought about when I woke up, and I was surrounded by family earlier that day. I self-harmed, right there, in my hospital bed.

The next day, a very unprofessional psychiatrist was sitting next to my bed when I woke up. I explained my story to her, she didn't even seem to care one bit. She just said she would give me some pills and send me straight back into that incredibly toxic situation. I honestly thought that was bullshit. The primary cause of my depression, my suicidal thought, my self-destructive behavior was due to the abusive parent I was living with, and she wanted to put me right back into it?

My mother showed up at the hospital the next day at 3am. She told me to pack up my stuff and that we were leaving. The receptionists at the front desk told us that she wasn't allowed to do that, but she convinced them to let us out. I honestly think she saved my life. My dad hadn't told my mother about what happened to me until a few hours before she came to fetch me, and she heard that the psychiatrist was just going to send me home with pills and no appropriate treatment, she couldn't let that happen. So, she decided to put matters into her own hands.

We went to her small bachelors' apartment that she was sharing with her boyfriend at the time, and she gave me snacks, and we watched movies till I went to bed. I found out recently that during that time, for the first few weeks that I was staying with her, she hardly slept a wink. She would stay up all night watching me to make sure I was still breathing. She did everything to make sure that I was doing at least remotely okay. She gave me anything I needed, listened to me whenever I needed to vent, and nursed me back to health. I will forever be grateful for what she did for me at that point in time. It's like she let go everything, all the toxicity washed away, and her maternal instincts just kicked in, she was my mother again. It was the one time in my adolescent life that I got to know my real mother without the drugs involved.

g. Where am I now?

I am okay now. I have had therapy, I have loving friends, and I have an amazing partner that pushes me to be better by the day, and listens to me when I need to speak. I am still healing, I am still getting better, but working through trauma takes time. I work hard for the new life that I have built for myself, and compared to years ago when I had no hope, I am excited about my future, and I know I will make something good of my life, even if it is simply just living life to be happy. I am so glad that I am alive. I am living the life I have always wanted, and enjoying every minute. Everything turned out to be okay.

If I notice the signs of anyone I know being toxic, I'll cut them out of my life before it gets any worse. I have learned to stand up for myself, and I know that not every disagreement will turn out to be an argument. I have the confidence in myself to say what I feel and know I won't be ridiculed by the people who love me. Learning to let go and only forgive if I want to, was the best thing I could have done for myself and my loved ones.

I enjoy doing things, I have aspirations and hopes and dreams. I know its not the end of the world if something fails, I will just move on or try again. It will be okay someday, I promise.

h. Things to learn:

- Just because someone is family, doesn't mean they can take advantage of you. Learn to say no, learn to stand up for yourself and make yourself heard. You do not owe toxic parents ANYTHING merely because they brought you into this world.

- Never lend a toxic parent money, things will get weird. They may never pay you back or will make you feel bad for even considering asking them for the money back since they expect it just to be a "favor".

- It may hurt for a long time. Healing is tough. Just remember to learn and grow from it. You wouldn't be the same amazing person you are today without all the things you went through. Get help, speak to a professional. If you don't like the first therapist, keep searching till you do. Not doing anything about the trauma you have experienced will never do any good. Get out of that lousy cycle you've been exposed to.

- Not everything is your fault: Stop blaming yourself for everything that goes wrong in life; you can't control everything that happens around you. You may be conditioned to think these things, and that's okay, but that's just something you have to unlearn after living with toxic parents.

- Most importantly, having toxic parents means you can use their mistakes and problems and learn from it. Learn from THEIR mistakes. That's one thing I always tell people. Learning from their mistakes makes life easier for you in the long run. You won't have to make as many mistakes as most people to figure out this wild and confusing life.

- Learn to love yourself. Life is precious, and you're the only person in this world that will be there for you, forever.

- If you want to forgive them, forgive them. If it isn't even worth the time and effort, don't. It is 100% okay to cut people out of your life if they cause you more harm than good. There is no reason not to cut that toxic behavior out of your life. At the end of the day, you come first before anyone else.

~~~~~~

Chapter 2a: Carly's Toxic Parents Story - Early Life

...What do you expect from a girl who constantly witnesses her mother being beaten like a wild dog by my drunken father?

The one thing that most parents cling to is believing that they know their children. They would swear that they know their children inside and out, but the reality is, they don't know anything. They only know what their children present to them.

After what I've experienced growing up, my biggest fear in adulthood and later in parenthood, is... not knowing that my child is crying herself or himself to sleep in the next room. My child suffering with depression, anxiety, low self-esteem, bullying and who knows what else. This scares me; the thought of, what if I am as out of touch with my kids as my parents were with me, because my childhood has not been easy and the saddest part is that my parents had no clue that I was emotionally suffering. Will I be as ignorant?

I knew how to fake a believable smile to my mother so that she would listen to me as I start to explain that I randomly get sad over past memories, that I'm unhappy with my life as it is, or that I'm tired of being mocked at school 'the girl whose parents fight all the time'. I mean, does it stand to reason that if she couldn't understand and reason things out with my dad during an argument, would she really listen to me?

She had no idea I was falling into depression as early as the age of 15. I mean what do you expect from a girl who constantly witnesses her mother being beaten like a wild dog by my drunken father? Or the nude cursing I'd hear (and occasionally see) from all over the house? Or the numerous times I'd lie under my bed and through sobs force myself not to make a sound as I waited for my parents' fight to be over?

I couldn't open up to anyone... What if they judged me? Laughed at me? No, I couldn't risk it. This young girl preferred to suffer in silence. I learned to be my own best friend... I remember I would pep talk myself like, "Relax Carly, you're gonna be okay. Everything will be fine. You're strong. You got this". I'd do this every time I was going through something rough because I was my own person... I had to be.

The more I grew up the more I became exposed to things happening around me. I really didn't understand how my parents would fight on a Saturday night and wake up for church on Sunday morning and pretend to be one big happy family. Being the only child of Mr. and Mrs. Smith - Mom being a member of the church committee - I had to be 'perfect' in the eyes of the rest... Faking was better than 'not being good enough'.

Church was the only thing we wouldn't ever miss... Not for anyone or anything. Even after my daddy left us - to God knows where - my mother would still show up to church knowing very well that we were the talk of the town.

Tracing back, this is where I actually learned not to care what people think and just do you. Period!

Chapter 2b: Teenage Life

My friends gave me a hug. A sincere hug. No one's ever given me a genuine and tight hug before and that's when I completely lost it and cried.

I honestly hated my father. I hated him for beating up my mother, for leaving us, for not having a better connection with me, for not being there for Christmas, Thanksgiving, my birthdays and for not being here today, on my first day of high school.

I started high school with a high set of ambitions for the future. I wanted to better my life and my mother's. She was all that I had now and after my dad left us when I was 15 years old our relationship got better. It wasn't a close one but it was better than before. We would at least have small talks and sometimes when I inquired from her why my father left us she would always tell me that I would understand why certain things happened the way they did only when I get older.

So here I was, planning my bucket list once I graduated and started working and making lots of money. From my point of view my future looked great. That was the only drive that pushed me to work hard.

I used to wake up very early in the morning to prepare my breakfast and get ready for my 20 minute walk to school. My mum was always tired and couldn't be up when I was going to school. She did 3 to 4 jobs a day to compensate the debts my dad left her to pay and also cater for our basic needs. It was a struggle for her and she needed to balance everything.

I understood and that's why I did everything by myself. I was independent. I was also an introvert.

I didn't know how to make friends so the only friend I had was my desk mate. Her name was Wendy. She was friendly and joyful. She introduced me to her other friends and that's how my social life started getting better. I interacted with her friends. We went to movies, parks and parties together. Every year we grew closer and I could almost see myself trusting and opening up to them. It was hard opening up, plus I still needed more time to be sure I could fully trust them.

Wendy would always go on and on about things that happened in her life and what she did over the weekend, what movies she watched and basically everything. I on the other hand would only give her the basic stories. I didn't know if I could go deeper with her or if I should keep it shallow. I honestly didn't know because I've never had friends before. My childhood was rough and I didn't know how to break it down for her and my other friends.

"Is your father or mother coming for the parent-teacher conference?" We were all seated at the cafeteria having lunch and Sally asked me that. That's when it hit me and images of my father started flashing in my mind like a tornado. Everything came up close in my eyes of him and the anxiety kicked in again.

"I don't have a father," I replied as I quickly got up and went straight to the washroom. I re-assured myself several times so I wouldn't break down at school. I knew I could handle this alone. I always do. This time it was different. A heavy load weighed down my heart and I knew every feeling that I had been repressing was screaming to be let out. My eyes got watery and I knew that all the tears I had been holding back were about to flow.

"Carly.... Carly.... Carly," I heard my friends calling me. I came out of the washroom and there they were, looking at me with sadness in their eyes. I didn't want this. I didn't want anyone to feel sorry for me. My mind created scenarios of everything that could go wrong and that's when I felt a body wrapped around me. Wendy, Sally and Naomi tightened a hug around me. A hug. My friends gave me a hug. A sincere hug. No one's ever given me a genuine and tight hug before and that's when I completely lost it and cried.

I cried in their arms and opened up everything to them. I told them about my depression and anxiety. How I miss my father every day. I told them all about the domestic violence I witnessed at home as a child. All the times I had to pretend I was doing 'good' when deep down i had died more than once. All the affection I craved from my parents as a young girl. All the times I cried myself to sleep. The number of times my own parents put me down and disappointed me and all of my birthdays forgotten.

I opened up.

For the first time in my life.

And they listened.

Silently.

Honestly, I felt better. Like a part of me had been freed. Like I could breathe again. I felt like I wasn't drowning on my own anymore. I had the best friends in high school. They helped me. They were there for me. They understood. They didn't judge me.

"Is that why you don't have a boyfriend?"

"Yes, 'cause my father was the first man who broke my heart before any boy had a chance to." I replied.

After my 'washroom incident' I knew the real meaning of a soulmate. A soulmate doesn't have to be the guy that you're waiting for your whole life. They can be right there, your best friends. The ones who can see how your life is messed up and actually stay and choose to understand you. The ones that won't judge you. The ones you can be yourself around and you don't have to worry about fitting in. The ones you trust the most. These are your best friends. Your soulmates.

Chapter 2c: Coming Out

When I came back, I found my mother home. It was weird because she was never home this early. She was seated at the sofa with the letter I wrote to her in her hands. Her face down, she began to speak...

Wendy and I were always together since we had the same classes. She helped me reject all the boys who tried to date me, and honestly, having someone stand up for you has never felt better. She was my backbone. She defended me in front of all the bullies who tried to harrass me in the hallway and make fun of my clothes. I admit I didn't have a lot of clothes, and the few I had, my schoolmates had seen them more than twice a week. They didn't know my mother never had the time to talk and know how my day was let alone buy me new clothes. I hardly saw her and we rarely talked. After school, I wouldn't find her at home and she would come back when I was already asleep. Weekends were her relaxation days and she didn't want anyone talking to her.

I spent most of my time with Wendy. She would come over for sleepovers. We would read the same novels and talk about them later on. She bought me gifts and always calmed my heart whenever my depression or anxiety kicked in. She was a hundred percent there for me. She made me feel warm and safe around her. She made me open up more. She made me happy.

See, I needed this type of care and when you are like me and someone offers a shoulder, you take it.

Wendy and I both felt the intense connection between us. It was becoming so intense that I couldn't keep it to myself any longer. That Saturday night when she came for a sleepover and we were laughing so loudly at 2 am, I told her. I told her that I didn't understand why I liked her so much. That I was into her. Not in a friend way. It was something beyond that. She made me feel things I couldn't understand. She made me warm.

I had never felt this type of affection before. No one has ever cared for me. This feeling of appreciation and a sense of belonging was so new. I honestly loved it and I wanted to tell her everything. Every emotion I felt around her.

I did.

For the first time, I was genuine about my feelings.

She looked at my lips and kissed me. I kissed her back. It was a special kind of kiss. My first kiss. I devoured her mouth as she touched my face with utter tenderness. Slowly we drifted apart for air after some time...

We were both shocked and looked at each other...

Her eyes gave a loving spark and she hugged me. She tightly hugged me and I almost cried. She had such a pure soul and I felt safe in her embrace. This is how I always wanted to feel and it felt right. In that brief moment, everything felt secure. I wanted to be this happy and when she looked at me again and smiled, I knew it. We both knew and felt it. Felt us. We didn't need any other assurance.

I felt at peace that night sleeping next to her and talking about random things.

When she left the next day, that's when reality slapped me in my face...

"I'm gay. I'm a lesbian"

How would I start explaining to my mother that I liked girls and was already dating one. It was too fast that I started doubting my own sexuality.

"Did I really like her? Am I really lesbian?"

I was so overwhelmed by all this but I also didn't understand why she made me so happy just by smiling. Her touch would be enough to calm my racing heart. I didn't understand how someone could make me feel so amazing at once. It was unbelievable.

I didn't talk to her for the next three days. I still wanted to be sure this is what I wanted. Her absence was almost unbearable. Like my depression was coming back all over again and that day when I saw her, I knew it. I was sure this is what I wanted. I wanted to be with her. She made me feel safe. I tightly embraced her into my arms and I affirmed my sexuality. She was my happy place. I kissed her and assured her never again to push her away. I changed my ways for her. I wanted to be better for her.

I wrote my mother a letter and placed it on her bedside table that morning. I told her that I was gay and that no one has ever made me this happy. I explained to her that this is how I wanted to be and that I still loved her. I told her that I hoped I wasn't a disappointment or made her cry. I told her that I hoped that she still loves me, even though I don't like guys.

I was worried the whole day. All I kept thinking about was how she was going to react. Either way, I had already made up my mind and I wanted her to support me.

When I came back, I found my mother home. It was weird because she was never home this early. She was seated at the sofa with the letter I wrote to her in her hands. Her face down, she began to speak…

"You are not lesbian. You can't ever be lesbian. I want to meet your husband. I want to meet your children." She sadly said, not looking at me.

"Society doesn't accept people like that. I can't accept someone like that. Do you even know what lesbians do?" She continued

Tears were starting to roll down my cheeks.

"Ma..."

"What will people say? No one in our ethnic is gay. We have customs and you're going beyond them. You will not bring me shame." She said with tears in her eyes, "Carly, you're not les.....bian"

"Mummy...... please understand" I cried,

"If you insist you're lesbian, pack up your things and get out of my roof!"

I felt the world crumbling down on me. The words were so unreal coming out of her mouth.

"You'll be lesbian once you're not in my house. There's no place for people like you. You're almost 19, so go and start your own life, far away from me. You won't even see heaven for God's sake!! I've worked hard to sustain you, and this is how you repay me? By bringing me shame? Leave like your father!" She screamed at me then tore my letter to smithereens.

I slowly crouched down the floor, shocked.

"Does God love me? "I asked.

Silence followed.

She didn't answer and walked to her room and banged on her door.

I waited.

Waited for her to change her mind. To come and hug me and tell me everything will be fine. To help me. To support me even though society won't.

Nothing.

Nothing happened.

I slowly got up and went to my room. Packed a few of my clothes and carried my savings and gave her room door one last glance before walking out.

I didn't know where to go. What to do. Who to talk to. I walked for a long time before coming across a bench beside the road and sat down. The words she said played vividly in my mind and I kept on asking myself rhetorical questions...

"Does God love me even though I love women?"

"If I die will I go to heaven?"

"Why can't my own mother accept me?"

People stared at me probably wondering what was wrong. At that moment all I wanted to do was to end my life. If my own family can't accept me how will society? Why was it so hard for my mother to accept me? It's not my fault I like women... I cried and cried till I couldn't cry anymore.

I called Wendy and as always, she came through for me. I rented a small apartment with her help and settled for the night.

I knew it was going to be tough but I was strong. I had already been through enough as a child and I knew I was going to get through this phase stronger.

I looked for a job and after several rejections settled to work as a cleaner in a restaurant nearby.

I graduated later on. I remember no one showed up for my graduation but I wasn't surprised because I saw it coming. Although I clinged to the 1% hope of her showing up. She didn't.

That day I chose happiness for myself. For so long I had always belittled myself, and maybe for once I could work on myself. Maybe this was the kind of energy I needed in my life... To prepare myself for something better.

The college I got accepted to was in another city and I was happy to move. To be far away from my mother. Maybe I will heal. Maybe not. But either way, I will take up the offer.

I looked up jobs online so I could sustain and pay for my own fees. It wasn't going to be easy. Will I survive?

Well, there was only one way to find out.

I was moving in to a new city. I didn't know anyone. No one knew me. This was God giving me another opportunity. To start again and achieve my goals.

I broke up with Wendy because she and I would be far apart and we both had some growing to do. Our relationship wasn't at the right time and we both mutually agreed to end it. I will forever be thankful to her because if it weren't for her, I wouldn't know who I really am.

She taught me love. She taught me patience. We weren't meant to be because life sometimes brings you certain people, even temporary ones, who are meant to shape you into better versions of yourself, to prepare you for a better future. That person for me was Wendy.

It was hard letting go on both ends but we had to do what was best for the both of us.

"Thank you God for bringing me this far. I know my next episode will be better than what I've anticipated. Please bring into my life someone even better. A woman who will forever be thankful to have me and accept me. Amen"

That was the last prayer I said before getting into that bus and going into a new city.

Chapter 2d: Adulthood and Finding "The One"

I had to choose my happiness. I had to focus on myself. One important thing I learned is that if someone really loves you, they won't compromise your happiness.

It was never easy. Life slapped me in my face more times than I could imagine. My head had created a very easy life... just working and learning.

Honestly it wasn't easy. There were times I felt like giving up because the burden was too heavy. I couldn't ask for help from anyone. I mean who? My mother didn't want to see me or talk to me. I tried... I tried contacting her. Leaving her voice mails, wanting to know how she was, but it was always the same. She never answered nor called back. None of my messages or emails were replied to.

I was tired.

The hardest thing I had to live with was accepting that I had lost her. Not to an illness or death. I lost my mother because that was the decision she made. That was honestly the worst heartbreak I've ever dealt with in my life.

College and work were not easy either. Studying for tests and showing up for work was extremely hard. Balancing the two was tough. But did I have another option? No... I had to suck it up and keep on going.

On the other hand, I've met interesting new people. Adult friendships are extremely hard to keep and maintain because everyone is busy carving out their lives. But it's so nice when they do pop up.

God's been with me in my journey. In this moment, I'm content with my life as it is. I'm slowly bettering it.

Throughout my life I questioned many things, including my sexuality. I questioned if someone had good intentions, if my friends were truly my friends, if my parents really loved me. I struggled with opening up to people and sharing love, love I never received as a child. It has really never been easy.

I've suffered emotionally and it took me a really long time to get over the fact that I'm not going to talk to my own mother again. I had to choose my happiness. I had to focus on myself. One important thing I learned is that if someone really loves you, they won't compromise your happiness.

Being lesbian is what made me happy.

I was happy that way and if my mother rejected me because of my sexuality, I had to be okay with it. I didn't want anyone else's preferences to determine my value. What right do they have?

I'm always making a vow to myself to never become like my parents. One day when I have children, I'll treat them better than i was treated. I'll give them all the love I never received. I will be part of their lives. I will want to see them happy.

I don't want my children to ever go through what I went through in my early life.

I'm going to give them so much love that I'll forget all the pain I went through.

It took me so long to find someone I really loved and to show her in more ways than one. To let her in and treat her right.

I admit that I've had a lot of doubts throughout my life, but I can name a few aspects that I never counted among those uncertainties.

I've never doubted her. I never questioned if she really loved me and I never felt the need to...

Her name is Lisa and yes, my life existed before we met but it's difficult for me to picture it anymore; there is joy here beyond what I imagined. I can't remember what my hands felt before touching her body or what sensations I felt before giving her my heart. It all seems so dull now, like there was little about my life that was spectacular before we met, her presence transformed everything. It has brightened darkness I thought was irrevocable and every day I am astounded that this romance exists; that I am regarded with honor, reverence and tenderness. I am so in love that I can feel myself soaring above everything that I have ever known. It is healing and restorative. It is a feeling that I deeply want to carry for the rest of my life.

Chapter 2e: Advice to Readers

Your current destination is not your final destination.

At this juncture, I'm talking to the person who has had a rough childhood. The person who has not received any kind of affection in his or her early life. The person who is suffering emotionally. The one who has or is still dealing with toxic parents.

I won't lie, this world is not going to be laid out nicely for you. It owes you nothing. It's all about how you handle things happening around you and how you react to your current situation.

Nothing lasts forever.

Your current destination is not your final destination.

Let the next few points I'll share help you through your emotional struggle.

1. DONT SUFFER IN SILENCE!

To everyone struggling out there I want you to know that:

YOU are allowed to talk about what's bothering you to friends you trust or to a professional. No matter how big or small the problem. If it's bothering you then it matters. Repressing and pushing down your feelings is not healthy.

It's not necessary to stay strong all the time. It's okay to break down, to cry out, it's okay to be this way sometimes. This doesn't make you weak. Venting your emotions will make you strong.

Life is all about ups and downs. It's all about learning from the worst and enjoying the best. So never stop believing. Believe in yourself, believe that what's meant to be will eventually find its way back to you. Stay positive and trust the process.

On the other hand...

If someone with any type of mental issue reaches out to you, let them know that while you might not understand what they are feeling, you are there for them and support them one hundred percent. Remind them that they are loved, worthy to be on this earth, that they were created for a purpose and that there are a lot of beautiful things inside of them. Be that person who isn't afraid to ask twice if they are okay when you notice a bit of hesitation in their voice. Just be there for them and sincerely care.

Trust me.

Don't suffer in silence.

Seek help!

2. WORK ON YOURSELF.

Please.

Work on YOURSELF.

There is a lot of time to be spent discovering yourself without hoping someone will fall in love with you along the way, and it doesn't need to be painful or empty. You need to fill yourself with love. Not anyone or anything else. Become a whole new person on your own. Give to others through charity or volunteering (your time can be just as valuable as giving money, sometimes even MORE valuable), smile A LOT, go on adventures, dress up for yourself.

Do all things with love but don't romanticize life like you can't survive without it. Live for yourself and be happy on your own.

Strive to be the best version of YOURSELF that you can possibly be, especially at a time when you have access to limitless possibilities.

You have two choices in this life: You can either fit in or you can become the person you choose to be. I want you to understand that no one is born perfect. No one starts out great. You are the person you choose to be; you are the person you choose to create. Choose someone great! Work hard to become someone you are proud of. Don't wait your whole life for a day when you have it all figured out. Take the initiative to create yourself.

We all have potential within us screaming to be let out, but it takes hard work and commitment to make it. Take the first step by working on yourself and watch as your confidence grows. Only when YOU focus on YOURSELF and YOUR worth will YOUR true strength show.

Be happy.

Genuinely happy.

Don't compromise your happiness for anything or anyone.

You deserve happiness.

You don't have to be like anyone else or pretend to be someone you are not just to fit the expectations of family or peers. You don't have to be anything other than YOURSELF.

3. YOU'LL MOVE ON SOMEDAY, I PROMISE.

I know that sometimes you stare into an empty space and think.

I did it often.

You think about everything that has put you down, that has been the cause of the sadness in you, that has scarred you and hurt you, how your whole life had been a mess. I know from experience how worthless and useless you can feel.

But I want you to know that this is life. It is imperfect.

I know it's hard on you because these thoughts pull back in the middle of the night and your past doesn't leave you. Your thoughts consume you and it's hard to sleep, so you keep yourself up because you'd rather stare at the ceiling than fall asleep and dream of the monsters that hide inside your head.

I know you've been traumatized and I know how much you cry because amidst all this chaos, you lost yourself, and more than all people who left, losing yourself causes the most pain...

That's why I'm here.

I'm here to tell you, you are going to be okay.

If you try. You'll move on sometime, somewhere, someday and you're going to find happiness.

I promise.

You will.

You're not alone.

We are all on the same ocean.

Just sailing on different boats.

~~~~~~~~~~~~~~~~~~~~~~~~~~~~~~

~~~~~~~~~~~~~~~~~~~~~~~~~~~~~~

Chapter 3a: Faye's Toxic Parents Story - Childhood

After countless tests, my parents were delivered devastating news – Diabetes Type I. Neither took it well, neither wanted to face facts so I had to (wo)man up and deal with my condition on my own.

I was born into a wealthy, influential family during the late 1980s. From the earliest age, my parents, my dad in particular, would drill the importance of my being born to a man who could pay my way. To a child of four, one who thought the sun rose and set according to Strawberry Shortcake, He-Man and She-Ra, Princess of Power, that didn't make much sense. I remember him complaining about shelling out fees for pre-school. My mother, the more nurturing soul between the two of them, decided I didn't have to attend. She was uneasy considering the man she married not only didn't seem to care enough for the both of us but had somehow managed to make her totally dependent on him.

It's odd how children can feel the tension between two parties. I can never recall a single day in my life where my mother smiled without the glimmer of sadness nestling behind her brown eyes. She was a much loved, only child to a man who had lost his wife soon after she gave birth to my mother. My maternal grandmother had decided that married life with a child was not for her, so she packed her bags 18-months later and cut off all ties.

My grandfather's reaction, in contradiction to my grandmother, was to create a world that revolved around his precious daughter. My mother neither wanted for anything in her childhood nor was she ever made to feel unloved. He saw himself as both father and mother, and she was loved madly, his princess, not the sun nor the stars were worth his little girl.

In hindsight, his overprotective nature greatly influenced my mother's own behavior and paranoia in later life.

During a business trip, I became quite ill. My father thought my mother was overreacting, and as usual, they had a huge fight. We cancelled the remainder of the trip and came home. After countless tests, my parents were delivered devastating news – Diabetes Type I. Neither took it well, neither wanted to face facts so I had to (wo)man up and deal with my condition on my own.

To comfort myself, I unfortunately turned to food. I became a carb addict and while I was not fat, over the years, my body fought to keep well.

Chapter 3b: Teenager

The first time my mother left to visit her family, we didn't see her for 14 months. Her family were angry that my father had abused her. Perhaps they felt guilty for not doing anything about it.

I had a rough teenage life, not rough in the ways one typically associates with teenage mishaps but rough, nonetheless. I had few friends, and while this didn't really bother me, my father constantly picked on my "anti-social" lifestyle.

He wondered why I didn't have the right friends, i.e., those families he would consider the right type. I was booked into a private school from early elementary school years. I was the only kid with a foreigner for a mother, and my classmates never forgot to pick on me for that, or that I looked different from the rest. My classmates would carry out mean pranks all the way through high school, and my father's answer for everything was, "Hit them."

The girls ran around in cliques, typical for teenagers I suppose. I buried my loneliness by hanging out in the library or bathroom where I'd read to spend the day. The last 2 years of high school were spent everywhere but at the actual institution. To this day, my father wonders how I managed to graduate.

I never smoked, drank or took drugs. For all intents and purposes, I was a decent kid. I didn't ask my parents for stupid trends (they wouldn't have indulged me, anyway), I loved sports and books, so I kept my focus on that.

The first time my mother left to visit her family, we didn't see her for 14 months. Her family were angry that my father had abused her. Perhaps they felt guilty for not doing anything about it.

During this time frame my father had moved us into his ancestral family home. I started seeing a different side of my father altogether. He was completely and utterly dedicated to his family. Issues, fights, celebrations, and more, he gladly indulged in every aspect of a healthy family life.

This puzzled me greatly for it was something I'd never seen. My father couldn't stand to be in the same room with us for more than thirty minutes, and yet here he was, laughing, joking, indulging in family love.

It was also during this period that I truly bonded with my sister, Alesha. We knew our parents were screw ups, we also knew that we two were the only ones who really cared about what happened to the other. This bond has only increased with time. My sister and I would die for each other, and for that, I am immensely grateful to my parents.

My mother's return just over a year later brought with it many questions, concerns and complaints. We understood her family were trying to help her regain her health, but Alesha and I wondered, "did you never think about what had happened to us when you took off?"

She seemed happier during her first month back, so our irritation melted away. But being around my father again, it took just three months to undue what had taken over a year, thousands of dollars, and two therapists to accomplish.

The second time she decided to leave, we were more prepared. We knew her "6-week vacation" would no doubt, turn into an 18-month project. My sister and I felt it was right though, so we jointly lied to our father who asked the very same question, when would she be back?

"Don't worry, she will be back soon. She has a Dr's appointment in 7 weeks' time, so she won't miss that."

I had finished high school a few months before her departure and wondered whether it was possible to go over and see her. Alesha was willing and excited at the thought, so we asked our father who denied this request. He said we can travel on our own dime at a later stage. Back then we thought he was a miser, we still do.

With teenage life officially over, I wondered what the next chapter would bring. Our ability to hope and dream, no matter the difficulties we face, is something admirable and definable. I hoped the next chapter would bring my mother, sister and I joy. God knows we deserved it.

Chapter 3c: University Round 1 (Mid-2000's)

My mother's weak attempts at trying to break through the bullheaded nature of my father never resulted in anything more than her tears and much sorrow that lasted for weeks.

Here I am, uncertain and unhappy. Most kids look forward to their university years, a chance to escape their parents' clutches, make silly mistakes, repeat them and so on. I had informed my parents that I wanted time off, so I could sort myself out. My mother was happy to oblige, and in a way, I understood why she wanted me to think carefully before I committed to any subject.

"Your father will be angry and hurt you if you waste his money."

English was my mother's third language. Her first being French, the second Russian. I grew up listening to these languages only spoken during my mother's conversations with her family. Somehow, my own tongue was partially influenced, and I grew up with an internationally unrecognizable accent.

"Mother, I don't want to go to university right now. I have no idea what I want to study. Please talk to him."

It didn't work though. We all knew it wouldn't and I ended up starting my first year without a clue.

"Don't waste my money. Study hard," he said.

"I am only doing this because you're forcing me," I replied.

"You're ungrateful. Do you know how many children would be grateful for this opportunity?"

"I'm not ungrateful, just unsure. I will attend after I figure out what I want to do."

"Do you know So and So's daughter or son are attending medical school?"

"I don't want to be a doctor so why are you comparing us?" I'd ask.

Somehow it always came down to money and comparisons. I kept thinking, "For God's sake, if you didn't want to spend any money, why did you have children???" It sounded ungrateful but the constant snide remarks, the emotional tug-of-war that ultimately ended in humiliation and despair. The constant reminder when a parent tells you that you are a burden really takes a toll through the years. My attempt at logic, the need to get to the root of the problem, was seen as impertinence and ungratefulness. If I asked "why" I was called unappreciative, thankless, ungracious.

My mother's weak attempts at trying to break through the bullheaded nature of my father never resulted in anything more than her tears and much sorrow that lasted for weeks.

"No Sasha, she is going to study. If she does not want to attend university proper, she can do it through correspondence."

I changed my mind three times over a five-year period. I was called out by my father for being useless and having no "staying power" but this uncertainty reflected how I felt. I finally settled down to study Psychology, and though I grumbled over the years at never "officially" using my degree, it has given me insight into people over the years. Motives, needs, desires – all were clearer to me. At times I am accused of psychoanalyzing people, and that makes me laugh. If they only knew!

Chapter 3d: Secret Family

[The acquaintance] relayed how our father enjoyed taking his son around, how they went everywhere together, and how involved he was, "It's really sweet, he's a wonderful dad." Alesha and I experienced a simultaneous bitter taste in our mouths upon hearing that. Who knew he had it in him?

My sister and I were waiting to catch the bus. We heard a familiar voice behind us and stopped to greet the saleswoman.

"How is your dad and little brother?" she enquired.

We looked at each other, shocked. In our minds, all the mystery surrounding his whereabouts, the unknown female voice ever present in the background whenever he called, a young child crying often touted as "your cousin's child", all of these finally made sense.

We confronted him that day. Instead of catching the bus, my sister called and asked him to give us a ride home. He grumbled but agreed to pick us up – we were scarcely three minutes away from him in our current location but in his mind, he owed us nothing and was going out of his way to help. It's always been that way, now that I think back.

"Father, Marion mentioned you're selling your home."

"Oh, did she?"

"Yes, she said you're selling your place. We didn't know you had another home."

"She must be mistaken."

"No, she's quite certain. She asked us about our baby brother, what is she talking about?"

And then there was silence. We repeated the question and waited for an answer though we had already arrived at our destination.

"Why did you do this? You made our lives miserable over the years and you had another family? Where is your shame?" sparked my sister. She was angry, more angry than I'd ever seen.

During the years, we had often discussed our parents. My sister chalked up our father's lackluster approach to us as "he doesn't know how to love." I had other ideas as I knew he lived for his father. That was love, wasn't it? I thought back on how many beatings he had given me over the years. Every chance to take his anger out resulted in him somehow becoming angry at me where I "needed to be taught a lesson." Did he hurt his new family? Did he terrorize them at the mere sound of his footsteps? Had they ever received a harsh word or look from him? Our conversation had lasted longer with Marion than he realized. She relayed how he enjoyed taking his son around, how they went everywhere together, and how involved he was, "It's really sweet, he's a wonderful dad."

Alesha and I experienced a simultaneous bitter taste in our mouths upon hearing that. Who knew he had it in him? More importantly, what did we do wrong to receive such shoddy treatment as early as we can remember? I was angry, hurt, depressed. The emotions turning in me were enough to drive anyone to suicide – something Alesha has often mentioned she considered.

We wrote to our father instead of calling. He had taken it upon himself to hang up on us if the conversation turned sour. Worse, his new wife, the same age as I, had been told we knew so she gathered up her kids and showed up on our doorstep.

Surprise, surprise, she held my brother in tow and was barely holding onto the infant in her arms. Our father had been busy, two kids and a wife forty years his junior. My sister railed at him, "You did this to us, and all the time you married a tramp? Look at how she dresses herself! You can see her underwear from here! Why did you do this? Instead of making things right <u>with us</u>, you decide to shack up with a waitress who cannot read!"

Yeah, my sister was really angry. The waitress literally did not know how to write anything other than to sign her name. Our father only found that out after they had picked up forms to fill out retail accounts. He asked her to fill them out as he didn't have his reading glasses, and she finally confessed.

We had expected him to ridicule this at some point. God knows my sister and I have IQs of 160, 149 respectively, but we were never good enough for him. This made no sense. A man who didn't know how to love not only gets married again, but spawns two children – for what purpose?

"Your mother made me miserable. That is why I stayed away"

"She asked you for a divorce, she's been asking for over 20 years, why didn't you give her one."

"I couldn't. It would have hurt your grandfather."

"Grandfather passed away three years ago, she was still asking."

"What's she going to do now? Old and alone at her age? No job, no friends, no life?"

"You prevented her from having these things," screamed Alesha. "You bastard! Where is your compassion? How could you marry a gold-digging tramp?"

"Alice loves me for myself."

"Doubtful, you told her you were a millionaire. That's the only reason why she'd marry someone more than twice her age," spat my sibling.

It sounded like we were being spiteful, but this blow was momentous and defining. He lied, cheated and schemed over the years. We slept on the floor in sleeping bags at our current home, he knew this but had never volunteered to help out.

Chapter 3e: The Beatings Stop Here

I should have felt proud for defending myself, but all I felt was the loss of a father, one who never wanted me. My heart wept.

I was tired, tired of being a punching bag, tired of being called stupid, lazy, imbecile. Crying, private or in front of him, never worked. He looked on them as a sign of weakness, he never bothered sticking around. Crying in seclusion offered no path or solution to the issues. I was stuck and could see no way out. I was still dependent on him, I needed medication and treatment. I had no family outside of my mother and sister, and both were as helpless as I.

Had I not been in such a fugue, I might have seen there were ways to overcome my and our situation, but the misery of it all just created a choking mist that never lifted. He was happy with his new family. My sister said we needed to stop looking at him as our father. He was just a sperm donor and I should think of him in that manner, or so she thought.

I couldn't let up, he had destroyed much of my childhood and poisoned my thoughts. How could I just let it go like nothing happened?

He stopped by to drop off some mail one day. We ended up quarrelling and he threatened me, "Shut your fucking mouth you pig. You don't know what you're talking about. I'm so angry I could slap you!"

I was tired of the endless circle of tyranny. I told him, "Go ahead. If you hit me, I'm going to give it straight back." He blinked and took a step back. I was 5'11" tall and had been studying martial arts for several years. I never thought to use it against him before, but I figured I should defend myself if he tried something now. "If you lay a hand on me, I'm going to break it. Do not touch me ever again," I said and walked out. He has never laid a hand on me or my tiny family since that day. I should have felt proud for defending myself, but all I felt was the loss of a father, one who never wanted me. My heart wept.

Chapter 3f: A Different Route

Growing up with abusive parents ingrains a feeling of guilt in one's mind. I had taken many years of physical and emotional abuse from my father so perhaps this allowed me to put up with my first employer's behavior longer than I should have.

I decided to try another route. Granted it was not my idea of starting a professional life, but my father's constant verbal abuse was driving me deeper into that dark abyss. We love stories where the underdog pulls through, where they make something of themselves and show they have a will of steel and courage. Cue the inspirational music, my sister and I decided I should try temping for a local business. I am well-read across several subjects, particularly health, and though I treated myself badly, I felt I had the skills to pull off the job. My employer agreed on the condition that I study the 2-year course part-time. I was paid a bad wage, obviously couldn't survive on my own but I was finally taking charge of my life, and hopefully this would be the road I could build a future on.

I started off working 6 days a week, 10 hours a day. The pay was abysmal, I was ordered about, required to fill in wherever I was needed. This extended my working hours but I was not paid overtime. I broached the subject on several occasions but was told this was how an internship worked. Since I was not qualified, I was "lucky" to be working at all. My pay, after taxes, roughly amounted to $250 a month.

I had known the owner for several years prior to my working with him, but I can conclusively say that after a year in his employment, whatever friendship we had was effectively ruined in the way I was treated during his employ.

Growing up with abusive parents ingrains a feeling of guilt in one's mind. I had taken many years of physical and emotional abuse from my father so perhaps this allowed me to put up with my first employer's behavior longer than I should have. I noticed he had a high staff turnover but decided that I needed to stay until I had finished the course and gained my diploma.

I was not unkind, and while he had acted like a boor, I came to his aid during the Holiday season when the last two staff handed in their notices without working out the remaining 2-week period. His second in command pulled me aside and asked if I would help. My own contract had ended on that day, and helping out would mean I would extend this another month and work the last 10 days of December, a time when many families, Christian and not, gathered to enjoy each other's company. In addition, the owner was taking time off and I would be required to fill in for him. I calculated this would double my salary, for that month at the very least, and I accepted.

As my father lived in the same area as my work, he would often see me walking to or from work. He pulled over a time or two to ask how things were going, this was usually done in the presence of his second wife who disliked my sister and me intensely. I was always polite but gutted.

He had literally thrown everything away, disrespected his family, and for what? This sounds very mob-like but my father's bond with his family (his five siblings) was never as strained as after his marriage to Alice had been found out. They refused to entertain any idea of her visiting them so he cut them off.

Chapter 3g: First "Real" Job

The idea that he had set either my sibling or me up for life was something we'd joke about. That taught me something valuable: never make assumptions about people, you don't know what lay behind their public masks.

I graduated with my diploma without lifting a finger to study. My sister Alesha thinks I'm an ass for never applying myself but, I reasoned to myself, I didn't need to. I received several distinctions and an A- - not bad I thought but I could have done better. A line I've often repeated in my life. I wondered why I hated studying so much. Then I applied to only one company; again Alesha thought it madness.

"You're smart but they don't know you. What if you don't get hired?" She was exasperated but, for the first time in my life, I was confident I could do this.

I had my interview, received a call-back and was given the go ahead to start next week. Both my mother and sister were proud, my mother especially as she had never held a job. I often think how she might have benefited from one.

"Things were different in my day. Divorce was looked down on, rich wives weren't meant to work," she tried reasoning to us and herself over the years.

I had huge plans for myself. I had finally done it – escaped from home …or so I thought. I was going to build an empire I could be proud of. I've been asked why I bothered working and "Do you do this for a hobby?"

No, I actually had to work. I had no trust fund as is typically associated with rich kids. What's more, my father had further divided our grandfather's inheritance between us and his kids with Alice. People wrongly assumed that he took care of us in that way, and he was happy to let them continue down that path. Alesha says he does it to be spiteful, trying to take away our accomplishments and minimize what they mean for us.

Every fault and mistake was picked on, dissected and discussed; in public if possible. There were many an occasion during my youth and early 20s where he would shout his frustrations in the supermarket or shopping mall. The idea that he had set either my sibling or me up for life was something we'd joke about. That taught me something valuable: never make assumptions about people, you don't know what lay behind their public masks.

Chapter 3h: Relationships

I hated the fact that people knew I had considerable connections. I would find myself asked for favors, invited to parties and networking events in the hopes that I could fix people up. I wondered whether I was liked for myself. It's a question I've often pondered throughout my life.

I met my first partner, X, during a luncheon meeting. We bumped into each other reaching for the water jug and he seemed polite and respectful. I hadn't realized how much I was willing to put myself through in order to forget the only constant male influence I had in my life.

I was in my late 20s, had a flourishing career, and finally decided to let myself entertain the thought of dating. My sister had always accused me of being somewhat shallow, and for many years, I wondered the same. Did I place looks before anything else?

I was still something of an introvert but decided to try being friendly and accommodating to those around me. X was nothing like the type of person I usually found myself attracted to. In fact, this was specifically the reason I decided to try and give it a shot. It took me 6 months to get into a relationship with X. I told myself that compromise was key in any relationship. While he was a good man, I did not love him and 10 months down the line I broke it off. He was angry and said I could learn to love him.

I hated hurting him but I felt like I was wasting both our time by pretending I was really happy when, in fact, I was neither here nor there. In my attempt at distancing everything I'd associated with being male, i.e., my father, I had inadvertently signed myself up for a relationship with someone I had nothing in common with.

I would become frustrated with X because he would take no interest in developing his mind. I didn't care that he had no formal tertiary education, but I couldn't stand the fact that I had to sit opposite someone who had no original thought floating around his mind. I didn't want a professor but, God help me, I couldn't stand another day being in a partnership where I was starting to hate both of us. X is married now, to someone who appreciates him for who he is. He tries to make contact, and though I've changed my number twice, he manages to somehow hunt me down. It irks me for reasons unknown.

I met Y at the gym. The gym, a place where many a relationship is formed and quite a large number of partners cheat on each other. My view sounds jaded, especially for someone who has not indulged in many relationships, but I had good reason. I was friendly but never overly so. I didn't do the dinner/drinks scene so I became known as the ice-princess. Y was an unfortunate trap I regret so many years later.

He was not flashy, appeared quiet, polite, handsome when you got to know him. I thought I knew him but turns out, he was the first serial cheater I'd personally know. Y and I looked like the perfect couple. We appeared fit, healthy, happy. I thought I had found the one, much to my delight, and without going through the proverbial number of frogs. As time went on, I realized that I had somehow taken over as financial provider. It's true we never lived together but much of our time was spent on my dime.

I didn't mind at first but the selfish attitude, the inability to not only give of himself, but care beyond a surface depth left me disappointed. In many ways, the more I knew him, the more he started resembling my father. Y was never abusive, nor did he shout. Instead, the cold, callous manner in which he conducted himself was cutting in a different way. I now understand he didn't care about me. He'd heard I came from a wealthy background, and perhaps he was hoping to ride the gravy train for a while until he found something better.

I hated the fact that people knew I had considerable connections. I would find myself asked for favors, invited to parties and networking events in the hopes that I could fix people up. I wondered whether I was liked for myself. It's a question I've often pondered throughout my life. At this stage, I have no one to question as I've alienated everyone possible save my mother and sister. I think I prefer it this way, no responsibilities to anyone aside from my immediate family. No need to invent excuses to avoid social gatherings. No need for pretenses of any sort. It's a lonely life at times but I prefer it this way. I can focus without worrying about distractions.

Chapter 3i: Therapy

Sheila asked him to list a few actions one considers doing for their loved one, small actions that aren't meant to shake your foundations but reinforce the care and consideration one expects from a loving partner. He couldn't name one, I wanted to bawl openly but held myself together.

Three years into my relationship with Y, I decided we needed to see someone. Thus far, I had discovered that he had cheated on me with a co-worker, not to mention numerous online dalliances. I installed a tracker on his phone and presented him with proof. He swore, he promised, he pleaded. He just couldn't stop his addiction.

Rather than give up on him, I brought up therapy. I knew a wonderful woman and had seen her on two prior occasions. He was iffy about attending therapy – he mentioned going to his church program for sex addicts. He tried it but he said it wasn't helping. I told him it couldn't hurt to try seeing my therapist friend, and reluctantly he agreed.

Sheila was the type of therapist who instantly set you at ease. Non-threatening, soft spoken, calm – her aura radiated balance and stability, something both Y and I needed. We started talking and she confirmed much of what I already knew. Much as I had discovered, she told him his constant need for validation meant he sought out random hookups in order to feel good about himself. He had come from a broken home, but his mother had the strength to seek a divorce and throw her husband out of their lives. Y's father was a drunken gambler who often spent their money on booze and casinos. They moved homes often when they couldn't pay rent. My heart broke when I heard this, but Sheila reminded both of us that his past couldn't excuse his present-day actions.

He started arguing that I was needy for attention and he couldn't give more than he already had. Sheila asked him to list a few actions one considers doing for their loved one, small actions that aren't meant to shake your foundations but reinforce the care and consideration one expects from a loving partner. He couldn't name one, I wanted to bawl openly but held myself together.

He sighed loudly and asked her what he should do to show me he loved me. She named a few things, all of which he said he couldn't do. She asked him, "Then why are you here? Why do you think you love her if you cannot show her?"

"My being in her life shows her I love her," was his reply.

"That's not enough. Right now, your actions are more like with acquaintances than a loved one. A relationship is about give and take. What you're doing right now is taking, and you keep taking without refilling the proverbial jar. A relationship cannot survive without both partners contributing."

"I can't give anymore at this stage."

"Then tell her that and decide what's your next move."

I hated him at that moment. Selfish and immature sprang to mind. I was accused of being judgmental often enough by him, and in this case, perhaps I was judging him. He wasn't ready for anyone, let alone someone with my baggage. It took me 18 months to finally let go. He actually protested for some reason, like we had a loving relationship and he couldn't understand why I told him to cut all ties.

I knew that much of the reason for this breakup was financial, but much as I still loved him, I couldn't stand this anymore. I had taken a long, hard look at my life. Didn't I deserve better? At the very least, I deserved to respect myself. He would survive, I needed to scrape my life together, but I had no clue how.

Chapter 3j: Resignation

I knew that the next chapter in my life would be a chance for me to completely let go of him [my father], to remove his presence and influence from my life.

After my dumping Y, I resigned from work. I loved my job but felt it wasn't right anymore. It didn't fit me, I was evolving. I had no clue what I wanted to do but this was the first step. My sister called me out, said it was bullshit and "what the hell are you going to do?"

I had no clear idea, but I knew I needed to dedicate myself to something worthy, something I could make a difference in. I had turned vegan a while back so perhaps that was a place to start. Animal welfare, laws and legislation, overturning a corrupt system on its ear. How to do this though – starting over when I'm almost 40, not something to take lightly.

I had no savings, no source of income, and could barely afford the place I was leasing. My sudden resignation was done impulsively but the need for change had built up over a 12-month period. I had thought about studying law since I was in my teens but never considered I'd be any good. I experience anxiety and stage fright when speaking in front of crowds. A surprising thing to note: while I never received any boost of confidence from my parents, I always believed in myself. That I could do whatever I set my mind to, regardless of how impossible it may seem.

My father received word that I was intending to study again and questioned my motives.

"Do you think it's wise? You're much older, why not go back to your old job. You need an income."

It was, perhaps, one of the first talks we've ever had where he did not aim at humiliating me.

"I think I can do this."

I explained why I wanted to study law, he listened here and there for a few minutes. I might have been discussing this with a complete stranger based on his reactions, concerns, etc. I knew that the next chapter in my life would be a chance for me to completely let go of him, to remove his presence and influence from my life.

Chapter 3k: The Road Back

Would I have made different choices had I the love, support and stability of a solid parental unit? I'm certain I would have...

It's taken me a long time to get here. Alesha calls me a "late bloomer" but who knows if that's true. The past four years, or what I call my entry into my 40s, have been a difficult period in my life. I received news that my health was failing on my last visit to see the physician. I have kidney damage, my own fault entirely, and will need to start treatment. I'm saddled with student loans and may never complete my education if my body gives up.

The bright side? I've finally come into my own. I know who I am. All the searching, all the doubt, all those moments where I asked myself, "Is this for me? Is there something out there I'm meant for? Is there something I was born to do?" These questions have finally been answered.

I've always been envious of prodigies, their certainty, that ironclad faith in knowing their path is something few of us are blessed with.

I've been envious of those with better health than I – having an autoimmune disease for 25+ years literally and figuratively cutting my life span down was something I rebelled against. Rebellion was not my friend and I did not feel good indulging in it. I did many stupid things, things which hurt me and my loved ones, things which seem stupid and petty now that I reflect back on my life.

Would I have made different choices had I the love, support and stability of a solid parental unit? I'm certain I would have, maybe not all my choices but perhaps the relationship(s) would have turned out differently. I know both were wrong choices, I knew it then but decided not to listen to my brain.

The first romantic relationship was a boost to my confidence – I was everything he was not, and he treated me like a queen. I was good to him but I never loved him nor would I have been able to carry through with that relationship for longer than the 10 months that it actually lasted.

I knew the second relationship reminded me more of my father, the better I got to know this person. I made every excuse possible. I hurt myself and others in the process, trying to excuse someone who had no intention of committing. I tried to force the issue and only humiliated myself in the process. I went into debt for this guy. I changed myself for him; ultimately, I failed myself for him.

Chapter 31: Toxic Parents

He was never willing to change; my mother was too scared and broken to change. Some people have a hard time expressing love, others have a hard time letting go. My parents were flawed. My father was never outwardly chastised by his father, my mother was spoiled by hers.

I always knew my parents had issues. They never bothered to shield their fights from us. I recall my father beating my mother when I was 2 – 3 years old. I recall him beating me at the age of 5 until my mother pulled him off me and bent her own body over mine to shield me from his belt. My attempts at trying to win my father's love and recognition were never noticed. My need to have a normal mother who could hold her own, never panned out. I had no one to turn to for most of my life, unless you count my sister, who was trying to scrape together her own existence. I look at them and wonder what they might have turned into had they been given a proper chance and guidance in their own formative years.

I don't have any kids, I want them but I'm not certain I have the health or stability to raise a child. My paternal grandfather would often tell me during my teenage years that my father was a fool for the way he treated my mother. "He has a good woman, but he is destroying her." My grandfather would not relay this to my father, and my father, striving to maintain his reputation as a great leader, would never bring this up to anyone. He was just as miserable but, from my end anyway, it looked like he could never muster himself to actually deal with the problem he created (that of having a secret family for so long). Out of sight, out of mind is something he holds true.

My mother still waits for his call despite him not setting foot into her home for 10 years. Alice snatches the phone away from him if it's Mom calling. She yells into the phone, "He's not your husband anymore, don't call here!"

Truth be told, Islamic marriages are dictated by a patriarchal overview. What was meant to provide safety and security for women has turned into an endless booty call consisting of aging men spawning endless children with multiple women under the pretense of honest marriage. What these men fail to acknowledge is that the underlying condition attached to multiple marriages is one simple rule:

- Treat all your partners equally, whether emotionally, physically, or more.

Not much effort there, right? Wrong! How do you pretend attraction to a 50-year-old wife when you have a 25-year old wife waiting in the wings? That's the catch with this rule – what the heart wants is not always fair or righteous. I've seen Islam accused of many things, and find when you dig a little deeper, the truth is usually easy to see.

My father discarded his ideals, his values, his promises because someone half his age looked his way. Or maybe I have it wrong, perhaps these values were just surface deep and meant nothing at all? Is it better for your parent to have an affair or "marry" again and again? How do you respect a parent that abused you over and over again? How do you respect a parent that allowed their child to be exposed to such brutality, yet blames you for the destruction of their life?

"I stayed for you! I thought children shouldn't grow up without their father, that's why I stayed!"

Asking either parent to look deeper usually ended up in a quarrel with me being cussed out. I've asked them if we could seek family therapy together. Naturally my father thought it thoroughly ridiculous, why would he need therapy?

That chapter is over though. He was never willing to change; my mother was too scared and broken to change. Some people have a hard time expressing love, others have a hard time letting go. My parents were flawed. My father was never outwardly chastised by his father, my mother was spoiled by hers. Neither learned how to deal with challenges in a normal way, something I hope to rectify in my own life.

Chapter 3m: Bad Parenting

It is true that I prefer being on my own at this stage of my life. I trust me, I rely on me, I don't have to worry about being hurt unnecessarily by me.

I'm no expert, and I don't claim to be. My journey through bad parenting harmed me in more ways than I can explain. Whether this was intentional or not, this did not reduce the overall impact over the years. The lack of empathy from my father, and the general confusion and moody despair of my mother created a never-ending cycle of abuse that impacts me to this day.

Parents imagine they always know best, that their experiences have geared them to prevent you from making the same mistakes. They think their word is law, and that any input from their children is neither welcomed or needed. At least, this was what I went through. I imagined it was the same for every child, and my father confirmed such. Only later did I understand that not only was this not normal parenting, but I was not alone in my toxic parent experiences.

The key issues in my childhood revolved around these:

- Lack of Support
- Excessive Punishment
- No Encouragement
- Excessive Criticism
- Constant Comparisons

I noticed that the last two affected my relationships with my significant others. While there were issues surrounding both partners, particularly the second one, I would constantly compare and criticize if things were not done a certain way. I've been accused of being a control freak, and in certain circumstances, I am.

The lack of trust due to my last relationship has created crevices of doubt where I fear entering another relationship could very well cause the same thing to happen again. My father, who had met Y, disliked him instantly. Whether he recognized a familiar soul to his own I do not know, but his behavior during my childhood created lasting impressions on me that have not faded.

It is true that I prefer being on my own at this stage of my life. I trust me, I rely on me, I don't have to worry about being hurt unnecessarily by me. I understand shutting oneself off from social contact is not healthy, and many will say they saw it coming.

I have always been a loner, and it is not something that bothers me excessively. There are times when sharing one's life can prove rewarding, I have not gathered myself again for that journey but perhaps I will try someday.

Chapter 3n: Strength

I heard a poem in my 20s, called "Invictus" by William Ernest Henley, and read it often during my 30s and will attempt to honor it in my 40s. The last two lines sum up the message: "I am the master of my fate, I am the captain of my soul."

My destiny was always in my own hands. I allowed many unnecessary things to happen, for better or worse. The saying, there are no second chances, holds true for some and slips by unnoticed for others. Life is not fair; nature or nurture can build you up or vice versa. For those of us who have been given a chance, any chance, at pulling ourselves together, it is up to us to be better than our previous generation. It is up to us to do better than our previous generation. It is up to us to be strong, compassionate, fair and worthy of our life. Blaming our past allows us to let off steam, to vent about the injustices we experienced - BUT - we should never allow our past to determine our future, especially if they have had negative impacts on our youthful outlook.

I heard a poem in my 20s, called *"Invictus"* by William Ernest Henley, and read it often during my 30s and will attempt to honor it in my 40s. The last two lines sum up the message: "I am the master of my fate, I am the captain of my soul."

From my understanding, being a parent is a responsibility that one carries throughout life. Whether you have born your children from your own body or adopted them, whether they live in another country or over your garage, parenthood does not vanish once your child hits the legal adult age. It does not dissipate if you sire more children in your 60s. It does not absolve you from those responsibilities a loving father or mother considers a privilege through the ages of their and your life.

Toxic parents are plenty, unfortunately, but we can do better if given the chance. Some say it's hard writing about your life, in a way I agree. You're forced to look back, analyze, agonize. Hopefully, at the end, you're able to hold your head high and say, I've come through this.

Well, I've come through this.

…And if my story is in some way a reflection of yours, you can come through this, too.

~~~~~~~~~~~~~~~~~~~~~~~~~~

Note from the authors and publisher: **Are you finding this book interesting and helpful? Would you do us an enormous favor and review the book so that others may see that it could be of help to them, as well?**

Thank you!

~~~~~~~~~~~~~~~~~~~~~~~~~~

Chapter 4a: Jennifer's Toxic Parents Story – The Early Years

Finally, my mother reached the closet. She stood there, with the door open, for the longest few moments of my life before slamming it shut again. "I hate you, you little bitch!" she yelled

As a child, I lived in a big, old dark brown house that needed paint years before I was born. I had an older sister, a mother who worked, and a father who worked so hard he often came home late after dinner. Our yard was small, fenced in not only by the old, rotting boards blocking the view of the back of the house, but also by creeping, pokey blackberry bushes that seemed to crawl on endlessly. This house was located in a shady part of town in the Pacific Northwest. We lived right next to a noisy train track and a college that looked just as dumpy as the rest of my neighborhood.

The interior of our house was outdated back in the 90's. The walls were dark, the windows were small and high on the wall and the bricks that made up our fireplace had begun to deteriorate and fall off. The only bright room, in fact, was the kitchen, which my great-grandmother Iris had painted a vintage pink color. They had been smoked in for so many years that the pink faded into brown in most corners, and the darkest corners of the house began growing mildew. It was shabby, but it was where we lived and I didn't think it was any different or worse than where the other kids lived, since my only friends lived on my block. I had two of those, a brother and sister close to my age: Adrianna and Diego. I was only allowed to play with then when my mother was visiting their father and we were absolutely forbidden to enter their garage; it smelled of cat piss from the outside. I spent my days trying to compare my life to theirs. Mine was better… at first. After all, I had a father AND a mother.

Growing up, I always had a fascination for learning how the world works. I wanted to know why plants were green and the sky was blue. I wanted to understand why we can only see so many stars at night, why there were nine planets in the galaxy, why humans were superior to animals. As a young child of only 5, I began my quest to start learning "why". I read books, learned how to use the newly integrated internet and studied constantly. My ability to read and retain information gathered praise from my father and other family members. My mother was unsatisfied with this, as her first daughter wasn't anything like what she wanted her to be and my mother figured maybe a daughter from another man would be different. Then, one month before my 6th birthday, she gave birth to my twin brothers. They were darker colored than my father, sister and I, and the months that followed were long, quiet months. My mother took up recreational drugs; the ones that turn your brain to slush. My father turned to alcohol.

As I cared for my new brothers and read and learned and played, my mother grew more and more bitter about my personality. In her eyes, I should have been the perfect daughter: wearing pink, glittery clothes, taking interest in play-makeup and going shopping with her. But I simply wasn't interested in any of that. My older sister, 3 years my senior, always said to me, "Be careful. Be quiet. Just stay out of her way". Unable to detect the fear and sadness in my sister's warnings, I simply obliged. After all, I didn't want to spend any time in the corner of the dark, old hallway labeled "time-out". My interests only grew and I quietly pursued my endeavors in astronomy and the way the world works.

In that year, my mother's resentment toward her children grew and grew. She didn't want or understand the responsibility of having four children; she wasn't interested in giving up her wild social life and unhealthy habits to care for her children. She stopped cooking, stopped cleaning, and dove head-first into the world of methamphetamines. Then, one morning after my father confronted her about her negligence to her children, she decided to make us toaster- waffles. We had been very familiarized with her outbursts of anger and madness and sat quietly at the table; my brothers in their booster chairs, my sister and I in our chairs with our hands clasped together on the table. We waited... then, "pop!" went the toaster. The waffles flew out behind the toaster and wedged between the oven and the pink, tar-covered wall behind it. We froze; waited for the screaming to begin. After a few moments, it did.

That was the day she began openly abusing me. She leapt at me in my chair, hitting the table. She screamed and yelled, "This is all your fault! You shitheads took my life from me!". My mother then grabbed me by my arm, threw me to the dirty, dingy tile kitchen floor and slapped me over and over again. My head hit the floor hard and I kicked her stomach to snatch a moment so I could get away. My sister ran outside; I ran upstairs into her bedroom, where I hid myself underneath the clothes of her messy closet. I could hear my mother's angry, rushed footsteps getting closer up the stairs. She was in my bedroom, across the hallway from the one I was hiding in. I heard her throw things in there. I heard her lift up the bed and slam it back down. I knew if she found me, she was going to hurt me again. After she was done searching my room, her footsteps neared. Boom. Boom. Boom. The floor was old; the house was old. I was able to feel exactly where she was. Once she entered the room, she began to coo... "Come out, I just want to talk to you. Come out so we can talk". Still terrified, I buried myself deeper into my sister's unruly pile of jackets, clothes and old blankets. Convinced she would find me, I piled as many articles of clothing and blankets I could find on top of me. I could barely breathe. I could feel my heart pounding. My mind was racing, trying to understand such a betrayal. Why was she doing this to me?

Finally, my mother reached the closet. She stood there, with the door open, for the longest few moments of my life before slamming it shut again. "I hate you, you little bitch!" she yelled.

Unable to understand why she was so angry with me, why she hurt me, how she could ever harm her own children, I stayed in that musty closet with my sister's rejected belongings for what seemed like an eternity. When, finally, I decided to test my luck and creep out, I could hear my father downstairs. He had returned from work, my mother filling his head with all the lies she had come up with to cover up her abuse. I crept down each stair, my legs trembling and heart beating so fast I though it would explode. Once I reached the door that opened into our poorly lit living room, I saw my sister sitting on our sofa quietly watching cartoons. She looked sick. Concerned she had also been hurt, I asked her to join me in the bathroom so I could speak to her without my mother hearing what I had to say.

What my sister told me made me nauseous. I learned that thus far, she had been my mother's only target. She had been to blame all this time for ruining our mother's life. She shared with me how she would have to endure the beatings quietly so my father and I wouldn't know. How my mother would only hit her in places where she had to wear clothes. How she would threaten to tell my father and hers about my mother's abuse if she ever harmed our brothers or I.

I asked her, "What if we told dad? We could tell him and he could make her stop and be a good mom again so we can all be happy!".

"It doesn't work that way, sis", she replied.

Unable to grasp the horrors before me, day after day went by as I wondered what I had done wrong to ruin my mother's life. After all, I wasn't even sure what that meant. My mother could do all sorts of things; go to the store, spend time with her friends, lay in bed and watch tv. She could do things I wasn't allowed to do, too. So why was she so mad? I began to wonder if the other kids at school had the same kind of mom. Doubting myself, I never really bothered to make friends I could ask. Did they get hit? How did they hide the bruises? How did they smile and laugh and play every day when such horrible things happen to people? Unable to sleep or concentrate on my studies, I, a girl of 7 now, stayed up every night listening for those footsteps up the stairs. For a long time, all I could hear through the vent in my floor was my mother and father arguing. My mother would call him a drunk, tell him he was a horrible boyfriend and father and throw things all around the kitchen. He would then argue that she was a horrible mother for what she did to us. He always knew what was going on; he just couldn't prove it. He began asking us to tell him when she hurt us, write it down, call our grandfathers. But every time our mother would hit us, throw us, pull our hair or scream at us, she would follow up with, "If you tell your dad I'm going to hurt you even more! I'm going to hurt your brothers and take all your shit away! I'll never buy you toys or feed you ever again!". Convinced that this would be our fate, we kept quiet. We waited and waited for a miracle but nothing happened. Every day for the next few months, we received our daily beating over spilled coffee, dirty laundry, or anything my mother figured she could blame on us.

Our lives went on like this until one day, a man came to our house who didn't look like the ones my mother was "friends" with. He didn't ask her to go into her bedroom while my father was at work. He didn't ask for money, or "stuff", or a ride to go someplace. He was a good man, a nice man. And he wanted to talk to my siblings and I.

Chapter 4b: A New Kind of Hurt

"That's mom's medicine. She takes it when you're at work so she can be nice to us."

The man that came to our house seemed to be very nice. He had a briefcase and wore very nice clothes. The man was called Brian. Brian came every week to talk to us. He asked us about our favorite colors and cartoons, about school, what we liked and how happy we were. My mother told us every week before he came to tell him we were very happy, we liked our house and we loved our mother. She wanted us to tell him that she was very nice and fed us and kept us safe, or else he would take us away to some horrible place. It was hard to lie back then. The Brian man could see that every time I lied, I would look at my mother. He somehow knew that everything I said was untrue and I liked him for it. Soon, he began to come to our house while my mother was away with her friends or out shopping or getting "stuff". We were still skeptical to tell him the truth; we didn't want to be taken away to some horrible place.

One cold evening close to Christmas, my mother was preparing us all to go look at the mall for things we would like. I got myself ready, my sister was warming up the car and I sat waiting for my mother to put the tiny shoes on my brother's feet. She hated doing that; they always squirmed and cried. I couldn't blame them; I wouldn't want her near me either. She finished wrangling my brother Jack's shoes on him. At three years old, he was so excited to go see all the bright pretty things. We hopped around together by the front door, waiting for my sister Marjorie to join with us. My mother, screaming at poor Benjamin to hold still, finally got sick and tired of fighting with him. She grabbed his right leg hard, slammed it onto the floor and began tying his tiny shoe, entirely ignoring Ben's little voice screaming in agonizing pain as she yanked his leg back into place. As she began on the other foot, his screaming didn't stop. Now concerned she had done something that would give away her horrible secrets, she rushed us all not to the mall, but the hospital on the other side of town. On our way my mother attempted to calm him, which was probably the only time I ever saw her care about her actions. When we arrived, she told the doctor she was a nurse's assistant. I knew she was, and it was only part time since she was home for most of the day and only worked the few hours we were in school. They allowed her to accompany him to the imaging room, where there were big, scary and noisy machines that made Ben cry even harder in fear. I wondered if I had that many tears inside me.

My siblings and I followed her and Ben loosely. I looked again and again for an opportunity to tell someone, anyone the truth. He didn't "fall down" any stairs and he certainly didn't fall down them sideways. My mother watched us like a hawk. She could read my intentions on my face, which she returned with that threatening look she would give us when she was about to do something bad again. Every time I thought someone might see that look, that horrible evil look in her eye, she would somehow change her face in an instant. She convinced all the doctors and nurses that she truly did care and she was so concerned for her son that she wouldn't leave his side. Unable to expose her, I gave up. The doctors told my mother that his leg was broken in three places and needed surgery. His tiny bones had literally snapped. That was the day I decided I would never lie to Mr. Brian ever again, no matter how bad the place was that he would take us. I figured that no place had scarier monsters or more dangerous people than my mother. I was right.

As little Ben healed, the days grew long and warm again. School was out, which forced my mother to put us in a daycare for the summer. Mr. Brian would visit us there and Marjorie and I would tell him all the things my mother had done to us as best as we could remember. He wrote all of this down on his fancy notebook with his fancy pen. He gave one to me once and told me to put all my dreams on paper. I saved that pen for a long time.

On a summer evening while both of my parents were home, Mr. Brian and a woman who dressed the same as he did came to our house. They asked to speak with my parents alone. I thought maybe this was the day when everything got better, that this would be the day that my awful mother would never get to see me again and I would go somewhere where I could never be hurt like that again. I could hear them talking through that vent in my bedroom that led to the kitchen. I could even see them. Mr. Brian's lady friend gave my mother a whole slew of papers. She said, "Mrs. Morgan, by law we have to remove Marjorie from this home and relocate her with her father. In accordance with state law, this home is unsafe for her as deducted by the school district nurse. We will allow her one hour to gather her things while you read and sign these documents." My father then spoke up to my mother, "This is your fucking fault. You couldn't get your shit together enough to stop beating your kids and take care of them every once in a while. I provide for this household and all you do is fuck it up and you've really done it this time. You are single-handedly destroying this family." Having never heard my father speak in such a way before, I was so scared I ran to my sister's room and told her what I heard. I cried and hugged her and couldn't let her go to that awful place by herself; I'd never met her real father before and it didn't seem like he wanted a daughter anyway. After they took her, I never trusted anyone again. Marjorie was gone for a very long time.

My mother was good to my brothers and I for a few weeks it seemed. She didn't scream at us, she didn't hit us and she didn't blame all of her problems and accidents on us. She cleaned the house and put all the empty alcohol bottles in the garage. Hell, she even cooked for us. I was scared even still. I couldn't understand why my mother looked so scared all the time or why she would give herself medicine like the doctors gave me shots. She said it made her a good mom and the medicine was to keep her from being angry. I was skeptical; under the circumstances anything she hid from my father was bad news bears. I learned about her "friends" that came by, how they would use her up and leave her alone. I kept quiet about all of that just to keep everything from going bad again.

One day, right after the sun had set (I watched it every day from my upstairs bedroom; it was the only thing I could prove to be real), my father quietly knocked on my bedroom door and sat down on my bed. I remember how sad he looked and I still can't get that expression out of my head. He asked, "Would you come sit down with me?" A little confused but unafraid of my father, I obliged. Presenting one of my mother's medicine needles to me in a sealed plastic baggie, he asked, "I found this in the garbage bin in the bathroom. Did you see anyone use it?" Without a second thought, I answered, "That's mom's medicine. She takes it when you're at work so she can be nice to us. It makes her really sleepy and we have to be quiet." My father then set the heroin down beside him, gingerly pulled me in to his side and hugged me. I thought I felt him cry, but he never let any tears run down his face. "Thank you for telling me that. I need to go downstairs to talk with your mother. You should lay down for a while and read, okay?" He said, then handed me my pillow and my book about the stars and quietly pulled my creaky old wooden door shut behind him.

Chapter 4c: Moving Forward

My mother always hated that, as a baby, I would only fall asleep if allowed to listen to my father's beating heart. To this day, I still yearn for the heartbeat of the man who protects me, although that role has changed.

Everything had been real quiet during the weeks that followed. Marjorie was brought back to me, which meant I asked her nothing but questions since her return. "What was it like? Did they yell at you or hurt you? Was the man really your father? What was your room like? What was your house and your school like?", I would ask her. She returned only short replies. "I didn't know them", she would say, and "I had lots of toys and things that I had to keep tidy. There were dogs. My father smokes and drinks like mom does". Having never felt that I'd gotten enough information out of her to decide whether or not she was better off away, I just kept asking. My sister just kept returning my inquiries with short replies. I decided it was time to leave the subject alone. I thought, Maybe I'll never get to leave anyway. Maybe this is it. I gave up hope that I would be taken from my mother and given a new family.

One evening shortly thereafter, my father skipped through the door in a rather cheery manner. Confused, my sister and I followed him into the kitchen to see what the fuss was about. He called for my mother, my siblings and I to gather around for the news. What he said was probably the most exciting yet scariest thing I'd ever heard. "Guys, I sold the house", he said. "We're moving out of the city into a nice quiet house in the woods. It'll be so much better for this family." I turned to my sister and she turned to me. We shared a look of fear and wonder. After all the basement floods, wiring fires and general hazardous nature of our house, we thought it would at least be more comfortable. And woods? Well, that was music to our ears! We all knew that my mother would never, ever follow us outside into the backyard. She would never attempt to chase us through our tunnels in the blackberry vines and through the hole in the fence. Eventually, she just gave up following us outside altogether. We must give her credit, though, for how fast we became as runners.

Our move was the quickest thing that ever happened in my life before. It seems we were finished packing and driving to our new house within a week. Looking back, it very well could have been, due to the fact that we took hardly anything with us. Not our china collections, not our records and tools, not even any furniture. It was bittersweet, leaving so many memories with my sister and brothers growing up, but also such a relief to leave behind all the traumatizing memories that shared the same places. Moving was a bit of a change for everyone.

When I first arrived at our new house, I had ridden with my father, while my mother and siblings picked up some essentials at the store. I was very close with my father. My mother always hated that, as a baby, I would only fall asleep if allowed to listen to my father's beating heart. To this day, I still yearn for the heartbeat of the man who protects me, although that role has changed. As we pulled up, my eyes filled with tears; there were so many trees, places to run and hide, things to explore! The closer we got to the house, the better it was: a huge tree right in front of the house, a thick, green lawn with ferns in random places and the one thing that made me happier than the rest…

"The windows! LOOK at the windows!" I exclaimed. They were big and plentiful, which meant that I could grow houseplants. I had always dreamt of keeping big, beautiful flowers in bloom all winter like my grandfather did at his house. My father smiled at me, walked me up to the door and handed me the key. I looked at him, wrapped my skinny arms around his neck, and hugged him the biggest I could. Once I was finished thanking him for moving us here, I put the new key in the new lock and turned it. The interior of the house was bright; the walls and carpet were white, the kitchen tiles were so clean and new and the cupboards were a light oak. Everything seemed like heaven. My father looked down at me and said, "This is our new home. We're going to have a fresh start here and maybe even be like a family is supposed to be. How does that sound?"

"Great", I replied. "It sounds great".

Just over a week after we settled in to our new home, my father got a new job. It was closer than his old one and he had more time in the day to spend time with his kids. My mother, seemingly in better spirits than usual, had gotten us enrolled in the local school. The town it was located in had a population of about 600 people, half of those being students at the k-12 school we were to attend. It seemed too good to be true. I grew to spend as much time in the surrounding forest as I could to build forts and learn about the trees, plants and animals that lived there. It was a whole new world for me, something I always fantasized about that really came true. When the first day of school came around, my sister and I were nervous.

My little brothers were a bit tense but overall excited to make new friends to share toy dinosaurs with. The school was a relatively large building; it had 3 corridors, two gymnasiums, a cafeteria and a fitness building. On our first day, all the kids seemed to be intrigued at the outsiders. I quickly made a friend, Isaac, who shared my interests and philosophies. In 6th grade, I never found many kids who had opinions about much of anything. Marjorie had endured a rough first day, as she was yanked into a mean group of girls who ruled the 8th grade class. My twin brothers, in first grade, had an absolute blast playing with all the new toys and meeting the new kids. We were all immediately introduced to the school counselor, who caught wind of our situation in our transfer files. I began to see her every day after school, where she helped me to talk about my trauma and see the light in life. Thus far, my new life had been nothing but beneficial. I even began to trust people.

Then something changed. The extra money from selling the house ran out and so did my mother's happiness. She had blown tons of money buying a new car, clothes, expensive alcohol and things she didn't need but wanted such as the rabbit fur coat we were forbidden to touch. She went from being the happiest I'd ever seen her to the worst in a matter of weeks. In order to stay out of her way and more or less under the radar, I took up hobbies that kept me either outside or in my room all the time. My grandfather on my mother's side would come and check in on us since he was informed of her abuse, and my grandfather on my father's side would take me to buy things to keep me busy. I began crocheting, tumbling rocks, growing crystals, gardening, making herbal teas and inventing things.

Most of my time after school was dedicated to these things and they made life seem not so grim. My sister started dating and my two brothers took to the outdoors any time they weren't at school. We did our best to stay away from our mother, who had once again succumbed to the dark temptations of the world's nastiest drugs. My father, although a hard worker and provider, picked back up on his alcohol abuse.

We all shared something to ease the pain, though. Since we moved in to our new house, my father had taken up aquatics. He had several large marine and freshwater tanks up and running within months of buying the place and even taught us a large bit about aquatic life and how to maintain it (I keep fish tanks to this day). This wasn't just a hobby for us, though. My father, included within my mother's radar of people to take her anger out on, found the tanks very relaxing. He would sit us down in front of them, tell us all about the creatures within and how they live, and allow the calm, rippling waters to lull us to a calm state of mind. It was as if my father had invented a new coping mechanism; a new kind of therapy. I ended up having my own aquarium, in which I kept a dazzling blue betta fish and his bright red girlfriend. This, in conjunction with many different sleep medications over the months to come were the only things I could rely on to rest at night. I began developing migraines.

The doctors figured, after I was made to tell them the truth, that my mother had caused me so many concussions that I had permanent damage and that I was likely to have migraines for the majority of my life, if not the rest of it. I started to miss school. A lot of it. I spent days wriggling in pain in the tiny nurse's office at my school, hooked up to tubes full of medicines at the hospital and inside big, cylindrical machines that could look inside my brain. My grades dropped, as did my ability to focus in class. I would have moments that were like daydreams, only nightmares. My mind would drift off to scary places I'd been before, like running from my mother or being caught in her grasp. I'd dream of seeing her running at me so drunk that she couldn't keep herself upright. As I brought these troubles to my counselor's attention, she decided to take action and send the Child Protection Services back to us.

This caused many more problems and many more beatings. I regretted every day that I told my counselor of the things that haunted me. My mother seemed to target my sister and I more and more each day, and eventually drove my sister to make her next move.

Chapter 4d: Solitude

The days came forth in a sluggish blur that debilitated all of us.

Marjorie spent a lot of time on the phone. This backed up the internet connection for everyone else, so she was limited to just an hour a day. Little did I know that was her most productive hour. In the time that my brothers and I had spent drawing up and executing plans to steer clear of the path of fire, my sister had been scheming herself. It was no plan to keep quiet and lay low so that my mother wouldn't notice her; it was a plan to escape altogether. It was a good plan, except it meant certain solitude for the rest of us. One sunny afternoon after school, my grandfather on my mother's side, Bill, showed up to take my sister clothes shopping and to stay the night. It was Friday; I had plans to hike with Isaac and my father intended to take my brothers with him on a cruise to the local hilltops, as he was an avid hiker and naturalist. As I sat on the porch watching my sister take her things to the jeep, I thought to myself, That's a lot of junk for one night. She's going to ask to stay again. A bit angry that I wasn't clever enough to make a move nearly as sneaky, I ran around the back of the house to retrieve my bike, which I would ride until Isaac's mother came to get me. She did, and Isaac and I hiked to a majestic waterfall beyond the outer edge of the town.

It was now Sunday, and Marjorie had still not shown up, just as I had suspected. Only her plan wasn't just to stay another night as I thought. That evening, my grandfather called the house phone. My mother answered, only to hand the phone to my father. I listened as I watched the corners of my father's mouth curl down. He put his hand over the speaker and told my mother, "She's gone. She went to live with her real father and there's nothing we can do about it. She staged the whole thing." Aware of my sister's plan, my grandfather had taken her and most of her things to live with her biological father, where she would at least be safe from my mother's unending abuse. The state, unable to prove the circumstances under which we lived (or tried to, anyway), could not remove my brothers and I, but Marjorie was old enough now to choose where she wanted to live.

Furious, my mother yanked the phone from my father's hands while he stood in shock and began screaming at it. Once she realized nobody was on the other line anymore, she threw the phone into the wall in the kitchen, damaging it and snapping the phone into pieces. I was mortified. Not only had my sister, my only support through this terrible life, left me, but I was next on my mother's main target list. I picked up the remainder of my sister's things in her room and closed the door. Nobody went in there for quite a long time. Life seemed to get even darker for us now and the days dragged on in an awkward silence. The alcohol bottles piled up worse than the laundry. We started to fall behind on our house payments and my mother had to get a new job. That was when it got really lonely.

Upon starting her new job, my mother also got a new boyfriend. She would see him after work on days when her schedule was scratched over and I knew better than the lies she would tell my father. Once he began adding up her hours and income, he saw the pattern. I remember their confrontation like it was yesterday. I could hear every word from the other side of their bedroom door, because it sat so high off the floor that my mother's weird cat could crawl under it.

My father spoke first: "Karen, we have some things to talk about. I need to know the truth." Having known about my mother's previous relations with other men, he was no stranger to this conversation. My mother, suddenly very aggressive, replied: "What is it this time? Am I spending too much money? Am I beating the kids? What is it now, huh?!" I heard a shuffle, and then my father, who replied simply, "No, Karen, you're cheating on me. I'm not stupid. Just tell me the God damn truth." There was some silence that lasted a few long moments. "Yes" was all she replied. I heard my father get up and the liquor cupboard by his desk open. Unable to move, I listened on. "See this is our problem Karen. You don't think about the consequences of your actions. You're driving me into the fucking ground. I can only deal with so much of your shit and this is just the icing on the cake compared to what you've been doing to those kids. You've fucked us all up and everything we've ever struggled with has been your fault. You either need to get your shit together and be a mother or just leave."

My mother, obviously in shock that my father had finally confronted her about her promiscuous endeavors, started weeping loudly. I could tell that it was fake; she did that all the time when we had to have meetings with the people who took Marjorie away the first time. I could never figure out where all those tears came from.

My mother worked her given schedule for about two weeks. Every day, she would take something with her; a bag, a lamp, some papers. I began to notice these things missing and not returning. I knew something was up, but I never thought I'd ever be rid of her. No way would she give up her favorite vice. She would never abandon the children she so very loved to take her anger out on. No longer shielded by my innocence, I caught onto her plan to actually leave us. I could never confront her; I could risk neither being beaten into silence nor getting in the way of her plan to get out of my life.

Finally, after two long weeks of watching my mother prepare to abandon the rest of the family and I, she pulled the trigger. She took everything that was hers and everything she wanted, leaving behind garbage and old clothes among items she didn't want or need. All she left was a note for my father, reading: "Aaron, the spark between us is gone. I'm leaving and I'm not coming back. Love, Karen". When I watched my father read the words, something changed in him. I could see a light fade from behind his eyes, withering away into dust. I watched as all hope to provide for a normal, healthy family washed away. All that was left were his two sons, whom he was aware he did not truly father, and I, his only true child, although we were all "his children".

The days came forth in a sluggish blur that debilitated all of us. My brothers would only play video games on the couch. I stayed in my bedroom with all my experiments and projects. My father began drinking himself to death and allowing the house to become cluttered and unusable in some ways. The bathroom toilet in our hallway broke, the roof started to leak and the kitchen was full of empty pizza boxes. He stopped cooking altogether and began feeding us only frozen pizzas, burritos and things of the sort. Because of our poor diet, my brothers and I found ourselves with less and less energy as time went on. I would sometimes clean the house or fix a meal from a cookbook in an effort to cheer my father up, which only seemed to work on days when he hadn't been drinking on the way home from work. Things were very grim. I felt truly alone.

Chapter 4e: Torn

I began to fantasize about ways I could end all my pain and suffering.

It seemed like an eternity went by before my sister Marjorie began calling me on the house phone. She told me how much she hated living with her real father, how they made her clean her room and do chores and finish her homework before she talked on the phone. Eager to come back, she made more cunning plans to have my mother steal her away and bring her back to live with my father, brothers and I. This began an entire series of life-changing events.

The plan worked. Marjorie came right back into our home and did all the things she wasn't allowed to do at her previous residence. 15 years old now, she was only interested in emailing her boyfriends, talking on the phone and putting on makeup. Marjorie didn't want to clean her room or do chores; I ended up doing most of that. This didn't bother me much, as I was just happy to have the company of my sister once again. Something about her changed, but in my mind it was just the time we had spent apart that caused the change. I was sure she thought the same. Determined to keep what was left of my family together, I endeavored to do the best I could to keep things orderly. I cleaned, washed laundry, cooked dinners and prepared my brothers for school each morning. I thought I had everything pretty well under control, except for my father's continuous drinking and increasing lack of interest in our lives.

That's when the day came that changed our lives forever.

It was a Saturday. The sun was out, the bees were buzzing and my
sister and I were visiting my paternal grandfather, happily eating a
bowl of goulash on the picnic bench outside. There were blooms on
all sorts of flowering trees and bushes surrounding the back yard.
The honeysuckle vine sent a sweet aroma on the light breeze that had
picked up and there were birds chirping from the feeders in the plum
tree. The cats in the yard had all piled around us to beg for food and
we happily obliged, just to watch them lap it up with their little pink
tongues. The clouds in the sky were white and puffy against the
brilliant blue that lit up the day.

Marjorie looked over at me and began to speak. "I have a secret to
tell you," she said, "but you can't tell anyone else." I expected
another secret boyfriend, a day skipped from school or something
else I didn't particularly care about. "What?" I asked. "Promise you
won't tell?" she insisted. Annoyed with her apparent desire for
secrecy, I obliged. "Fine, I promise" I said. My sister sat down her
food, looked me in the face, and said: "Dad raped me."

I choked on my food and dropped my bowl.

"Are you serious?" I asked. She must be lying. He would never think
of doing something like that. My sister had accused men of this
before, namely my mother's secret lovers.

"Yes," she replied, "Lots of times. All the times when you were
gone. He let me smoke weed and drink vodka with him too. It made
me feel really tired and loopy.".

Disgusted, betrayed and sunk to a deep level of despair, I broke my
promise. I ran into my grandfather's house without taking off my
shoes and blurted the news out to him. Absolutely enraged, he
immediately called my mother to ask the meaning of this. That
horrible woman I had grown to hate drove to the house to retrieve
my sister and talked to my grandfather in the house for what seemed
like hours. Finally, she and my sister left, once again, without me.
Over the next 24 hours, my grandfather, a man of honor, mulled over
what to do with the information he had.

He finally came to the conclusion that, whether or not it really happened, the courts would find out the truth. He called the police, who went to my home and took my father away. He left a tape measure on the base of a new fish tank he was building, open and marked where the glass would go. I remember how empty the house seemed then. The only person in my life I trusted vanished, unable to care for me any longer.

Arrangements were made for my brothers and sister to stay with my mother and her new boyfriend, who I had never met. They would have weekly examinations to ensure they were not being mistreated. My mother was forced to take urinalysis tests just as often in order to keep them in her custody. Regular wellness checks were made, along with random drop-ins from state officials. I, on the other hand, was promoted by the rest of my family to stay with my grandfather, who was legally my extended relative. After a few weeks, he legally adopted me as his own and my mother signed all of her rights to me over to my grandfather. I was lonely, but happy to be safe. My grandfather soon became the only person in the world I trusted, besides my friend Isaac, who had been listening to me and giving me advice about how to cope with my troubles.

My grandfather began to rehabilitate me once the depression set in. I had been in a state of shock since the day my family fell apart, unable to eat much or keep interest in school. I rarely left the house except to walk in the woods and think. I was put into counseling outside of school and prescribed antidepressant drugs which only seemed to promote episodes of mania, then followed by all sorts of other drugs to find the one that worked for me. This was a seemingly endless process until I was prescribed the first anti-depressant, which essentially turned me into a zombie. All my previous dabbling in art, writing and poetry seemed to fade away. I became a vegetable, only leaving my bedroom and my headphones to go to school. I began sleeping late, missing parts of school days and eventually whole days altogether. My doctors didn't know the best course of action to take, so I was taken off of that anti-depressant and prescribed another.

That one, at age 15, was probably the worst idea my doctor ever had. I became dependent on the drug, taking higher doses than I was meant to and going days without eating or drinking anything. I had a hard time doing anything that required energy and eventually gave up my hobbies. I became paranoid, unapproachable and generally exhausted. My dreams turned into nightmares reenacting my sister's gruesome accusations that echoed through my head all day and night. I would hallucinate my mother's face in my bedroom window and hear her footsteps behind me in the hallway at night. It was a nightmare I couldn't escape, no matter how much medication I took. This path took me to my darkest days.

I began to fantasize about ways I could end all my pain and suffering. My family never contacted me, my friends began to fade away and I rarely attended school. I tried all sorts of methods to control my pain; I cut myself to give myself the illusion that I was in control of my suffering, I attempted to overdose on my medications and I spent countless cold days in the forest hoping I would freeze to death. I considered jumping off the bridge over the river in the winter, hopping into it from the bank above near the house, and lying down on the highway in front of the house to wait for a log truck to squish me. I would look for my grandfather's guns and try to piece them together to no avail. I took up smoking in hopes that it would give me cancer, only to stunt the growth of my lungs. Eventually I began drinking alcohol and smoking pot; they were the only things that provided temporary relief from all the trauma I had endured and the nightmares that came with. Then, when I was 14 years old, the girl who was soon to be my best friend transferred to my school.

Chapter 4f: A Like Mind

It was a preposterous idea… I'd never seen her feel guilt for anything she'd ever done before.

This girl had a wild hairdo. Where I lived, nobody had brightly colored hair or wore shoes that didn't tie. There were no beat up band hoodies or wallet chains. This girl had all that going on, which immediately drew my attention to her. I introduced myself the first day and she invited me to go home with her and meet her mother. I called my grandfather to tell him I had made a friend and I was going to her house to meet her family and hang out. He was delighted to hear that I was going to do something social and agreed to pick me up later that evening. Kylie lived just a couple blocks away from the school, a distance I didn't mind walking in the rain. After all, it rained almost all year here anyway.

When we arrived at her house, I was introduced to her mother, brother, aunt and uncle and then shown to Kylie's room, where she had all of her things already organized and unpacked. She had posters of bands, random collections of road accessories like reflectors and traffic cones, all kinds of skate shoes and clothes, makeup and a variety of pipes and bongs that sat on her bedside table. She asked me if I had smoked weed before and, after quickly explaining my situation, we shared our first day together. Kylie also smoked cigarettes, which was something I wasn't particularly fond of. That soon changed when I asked her for one on the day that my mother called me for the first time in over a year.

When my mother and I spoke over the phone, it was aggressive. She attempted to apologize for all the things she had said and done and for my father being taken from me so abruptly. I couldn't forgive her. She didn't deserve to be free of what she did to me. Hell, she didn't even deserve to speak to me. As far as I was concerned, I didn't ever want to speak to her again and I intended not to. After that phone call, I was through with her.

My siblings and I, however, remained in contact with each other after that. We joined a social media website so we could easily message each other and keep up with our lives. I learned that my mother's new boyfriend forbade her from harming my siblings and threatened to kick her out onto the street if he ever found out she did. He made a strong effort to raise my brothers with morals and respect and even turned my sister around after she fell into drinking habits with my mother.

This man, Marcus, had even invited me over for holiday meals. It was actually really weird that she had chosen a man with standards. Unable to believe my mother was living with such an influence, I decided to go one Christmas the year I turned 14. Their house was decorated and my brothers had grown so much I almost didn't recognize them. My sister had cleaned up her act and no longer looked like the mess she was following the events that happened before. Everyone seemed happy, until dinner came along.

My mother, just as she had every year, managed to burn the gravy and a casserole. Expecting her to lash out at me, I hid in the bathroom, waiting for the screaming to blow over. But, instead of screaming, she simply cried in defeat, the pitiful tears running down her face as her boyfriend held her and told her not to worry, everything looked delicious.

I could hear her say, "I can't do anything right. This is just what I get for trying so hard to have a nice dinner." And Marcus would chime in, "Don't worry honey, it's just food. Just because it doesn't look perfect doesn't mean it doesn't taste perfect."

Amazed and a bit shocked, I emerged from the bathroom. I couldn't believe that my mother, the woman who beat me, degraded me and hated me, was crying actual tears in front of me instead of threatening my life. The rest of the night went well after she made another pot of gravy and I returned home to my grandfather, where he awaited my review of the evening.

I told my grandfather of the strange behavior my mother had shown. He seemed equally as surprised as I; it was unlike my mother not to entirely destroy a family holiday. It was as if a switch had been turned off, or on, or whichever way made her convey actual emotion. I thought maybe that this man that she abandoned her children and their father to be with could have awoken some sense of guilt inside her. It was a preposterous idea; after all, I'd never seen her feel guilt for anything she'd ever done before.

Unable to make a connection, I consulted my new best friend, Kylie, who had similar family problems, only not so violent. She thought that maybe, after all this time, her human mind would just no longer allow her to live with the thoughts of all the terrible crimes she'd committed. She suggested that her "mean bulb" just burned out, and her human desire to live and function in a family setting took over. Whatever the case, we both decided that my mother still deserved neither to be trusted nor forgiven for her actions. I knew even then that what I endured, what my entire family endured, would haunt us for years to come.

As the days came and went, I spent more and more time with Kylie. She had a like mind. I could tell her anything and she would have an experience similar to it. Her personality was unlike mine at first, however, because she was much stronger than I. When something happened to her, she knew what to do. When someone crossed her, she knew what to do. She'd been raised in a city, where problems like mine were far more common than where we lived now, so she had a solution for just about every problem that came her way.

I guess she wore off on me after a while. I soon began to face my problems instead of hiding from them. I didn't let kids at school talk down to me or make me feel "weird" or "different". I colored my hair a bright neon red and kept it that way for a long time. I wore clothes that I liked and shoes that came all the way up to my knees with laces. I must have been a sad sight, because I would always be confronted by my teachers, asking if I was okay or if I needed anything.

As the weather got colder and I bundled up more, I could feel myself slipping back into my sad, quiet self. My grandfather took me back for counseling in an attempt to help. It didn't, really, because anymore I was just repeating myself. The only things that made me feel better were art and music, and I had gotten pretty good at drawing in all the time spent alone in my room. My happy place was simply lying on my bed with my Pink Floyd CD in the player and a pencil in my hand. I would experiment with markers, pens, and paint, but something about the way graphite created images so perfectly kept me buying new pencils and sketchpads. I'd fill about one of those per week and then compare them to older ones.

I could see my development over time, but I kept noticing a pattern in all my art. No matter what, somewhere, there was always an eye in the picture. My counselor theorized that maybe this was because I had an actual eye that didn't work, and so I would create what I wished I had on paper. I found this to be partially true, as I would draw beautiful scenes in nature and peculiar plants and flowers. I even still hold skin on Kylie's arm; she had a portion of one of my drawings protesting the war on nature tattooed on her right forearm so she'd always remember me no matter where her family dragged her next.

I gave lots of my art to Kylie. She kept them in a scrapbook, on her walls and even some in frames downstairs. She loved it, and I loved her ability to keep them flowing out of me. It seemed like she was full of inspiration and ideas, just waiting to transfer into the right mind. We created all sorts of interesting things together, even an attempt at a calendar full of psychedelic drawings of mushrooms, tiny people and, of course, eyes. That project failed, but we had fun just smoking, relaxing and coming up with hilarious ideas for weird art that nobody would ever understand but us. My art even became briefly popular at our school; kids would ask for drawings to hang on their lockers, teachers would ask for drawings to hang near their desks.

I enjoyed the connection, but I also knew that I was very unlike my admirers and that drawing alone wasn't filling the void I so wished to plug. So, one night while staying over with Kylie, I had a dream that I was on a stage, playing a guitar. I could see my fingers moving on the frets and hitting all the strings at the right time. This dream turned into another of my endeavors.

Chapter 4g: Turnaround

I found out shortly after the 2-month mark of my own motherhood that my mother hadn't actually changed on her own; her brain was simply fried.

My grandfather and I had been driving to guitar lessons for some time now. Within weeks of starting, I was already serenading my grandfather in the truck on our way home from lessons. My teacher, Dave, told of how I had a natural talent and I was his prodigy. This kept up for years. The first year, however, was when I was put onto a real stage in front of real people to play a duet with another kid who took lessons. It was our first Christmas recital.

Dave, having the same taste in music as I did although he was a little older than my father, picked my favorite song ever: "Wish You Were Here", by Pink Floyd. This song resonated within me; I had every note, every scratch of the strings in that song memorized. The recital went so well that our director received donations to buy more instruments for the studio. It was a wonderful year.

I didn't invite my mother.

Months and months went by without speaking a word to her. My "musical therapy" seemed to be working, and I even went on to buy two guitars of my own. I would play every night until my fingers bled and then, once they stopped bleeding from all the calluses, I'd fall asleep with my guitar in my lap. My grandfather made me a studio out of the room attached to the garage, as it was well insulated and relatively soundproof. This was where I let everything go; all my feelings and emotions, my troubles and dreams, even my hopes for the future flew around in the atmosphere of that room at one point or another.

Then, when I was 16 years old, my father was released from jail. My grandfather had found evidence supporting my father's innocence and proceeded to post his bail. He hadn't been tried for crimes yet, however, as the system seemed to fall into one "complication" or another during his time in the hole. What my grandfather found was that my sister's claims of abuse had dates on them; dates that didn't add up. He would have been tried for committing a crime during a time when my sister Marjorie didn't even live with us. That raised suspicion among my family, as Marjorie had been similarly "abused" by men my mother no longer wished to have relations with. We'd caught on to my mother's agenda and she was not happy to receive this news. I called her that night for the first time in a long time.

"Hello?" She asked from the other line. "Hello Mother." I blankly replied.

"You haven't called in a long time", She said. "I know, Mother."

I couldn't hold back my anger. For the first time ever, I really blew up at her. It seemed like my pain was an explosive waiting to go off in the right direction all these years and now was my chance. I seized the moment and let go.

"You know what? I know about your stupid little plan to get my father thrown in jail so you don't feel responsible for ruining his life, but guess what? We're onto your little fucking plan now and we're not holding back. You trashed my whole fucking life and Marjorie's and Ben's and Jack's too and all you EVER cared about was yourself. You were so fucking selfish that you were willing to let a human ROT in a CELL for shit YOU KNOW he didn't do!! Fuck you, I hope you go to prison for lying right into the face of the law. Go to Hell and don't ever even think about trying to have a relationship with me ever again because when it mattered most, you didn't give a shit. Bye."

I didn't want to hear what she had to say. I felt like her voice would make me sick if I heard it one more time. I knew that this was within her abilities and she would use my sister as a buffer if she had to. Hell, she'd probably use any one of us a body shield if anyone ever got the good heart to shoot at her.

The lawyer we hired for my father was good and even went on to be a prosecuting attorney after our case. Although my father wasn't allowed communications with any minors, which included his own daughter, we managed to signal each other through silly code names over the phone in my grandfather's voice. He would tell me, "Elmo says that he would tell you happy birthday, but he can't, so he won't" with a smile on his face. Still unsure of what actually happened, I would play along, but I knew someone would burn for what happened to my family; it's just the way the world was. I wanted it to be my mother. Or my sister. Anyone but the only man who tried to give me a good life when I was a child.

We went to court with the evidence we had, but they were uninterested. In their eyes, a scared little girl was hurt and somebody had to pay for it. But I knew my mother, and I knew my sister. My mother was a scheming, lying pile of shit and my sister was so gullible she'd sleep on a railroad if someone told her she would wake up refreshed. Marjorie had been used. Not once, but several times, and not by any man. My father was sentenced to 9 months in the county jail and probation for life. I didn't do anything except play my guitar it seemed for the entirety of the sentence.

My father was released during my senior year of high school. I transferred to an alternative school that only required me to attend twice a week so I could graduate. My grades had dropped tremendously since the sentencing and I was reduced to a zombie that only played Pink Floyd songs and smoked pot. In May, I turned 18 years old; old enough now to visit my father without any restrictions. After years of separation, I barely knew my father, and he barely knew me. At first, it was awkward. We didn't know what to talk about except the terrible things that took hold of our lives. His happiness for his freedom was short lived, however, and he became depressed about his probation sentence. He was stuck in possibly the worst county in our state and I couldn't blame him for being miserable. Unable to handle the sorrows of us both, I distanced myself from him. My mother began trying to make up for what she had done. She gave me a car, helped me pay the bills in my new apartment and listened to my problems. It seemed as if she really had recovered.

I found out shortly after the 2-month mark of my own motherhood that my mother hadn't actually changed on her own; her brain was simply fried. Her Marcus had passed away of kidney disease two years prior to our interaction, and she had found herself a new boyfriend, this one straight from the bottom of the gutters. He reintroduced her to meth, gave her a disease and led her straight back down the path of alcoholism. Her brain was so toasted that she couldn't be abusive even if she wanted to; she didn't have the capacity for it.

Marjorie was now living with her fiancé and working while my brothers were living safely with an old friend of my mother's. She and her boyfriend shared a trailer together in the armpit of the town she lived in. For the first time in my entire life, my mother had a genuine look of peril when I told her of my stresses and complications. She even looked guilty as I explained what she had done to my father, how she'd ruined his life. If a stranger looked at her, he would see a helpless housewife with a craving for malt liquor. It was a transition that took some time for me to make, as I'd never had a mother figure before and I was still rather bitter about my childhood.

Chapter 4h: The Side Effects

Hang onto things in life that make you happy and don't let them go until you realize that it is pointless to be sad or to carry around your pain.

Several years went by and I kept a loose relationship with both parents. My father would take me out to coffee frequently and show me all his cool new hobbies and even found himself a girlfriend. She was nice, but she had a bit of a drinking problem. Nonetheless, they went hiking together and both lived in trailers, so they had some things in common. My mother would invite me over for dinner sometimes and we'd listen to music and talk. She was never the same person after her meth episode; she was a more simple, defined person now. What you saw was what you got, like a blank piece of paper. She had an empty stare and most of her teeth had fallen out, but she never showed me hostility ever again. I never did forgive her, but I chose to stay in contact anyway, mostly out of pity for what she had done to herself. She'd never remember all the things she did when I was growing up and frankly I didn't think she had the capacity to. You can't punish a dog for something it did yesterday.

I worked right out of high school. At age 20, I had a work accident that changed the way I worked permanently. On a hot summer day, I was doing my job cutting up a broken pallet for recycling with my circular saw. It was what I did every day, only this day was different. I didn't take my first break, and the night before I stayed late to catch up. Exhausted, I lost the use of my arm for a split second with my saw running. In a flash, everything changed. Things went fuzzy; the only other girl in the place ran to me, screaming for help. The scrawny guy in charge of the area looked down at my leg, and so did I; there was a huge, gaping hole in the middle of my thigh. Blood poured out of it, and the surrounding tissue was covered in wood shavings. It didn't hurt. My supervisor, Kevin, tied his t-shirt around my laceration, which ultimately saved me from bleeding out. I was rushed to the hospital in an ambulance, where I vowed I would never be stuck with a needle again. They stitched me up with 3 layers of suture and sent me on my way.

I left with no medication. The next morning, my mother picked me up and took me to my pharmacy. I immediately took enough pills to sleep all day; I had just spent all night feeling everything. In the following weeks, my mother visited me often to help me shower or bring me food and medication. My father sent me emails of cute animals and pictures from the tops of the hills where I used to live. I recovered quickly and was running on the 5th week after the accident. My parents had never been so supportive of me before, so I believe still that seeing their child in pain made them realize things about themselves as parents.

Three years went by. Then, about a year ago, I went to the hospital in an immense amount of pain that had been building. I had a migraine for about a week at that point, my insides felt like knives were in them and I could barely walk. I left work, promising to make up my time the following week. The doctors did scans, blood tests, physical tests and asked me tons of questions. It was decided that I wasn't leaving that night.

I was diagnosed in the following weeks with Fibromyalgia, Endometriosis, Intestinal Permeability and Hypoglycemia. I had gallstones, ovarian cysts and stomach ulcers. The professionals wondered how I'd gone so long just suffering without any medication. I told them pain has little hold on me, and how I'd survived as a child through so much turmoil and pain. My doctor told me that all these conditions are linked to stress and trauma; that I likely developed them long, long ago when I first started having migraines as a child. He told me that I was so traumatized by the things in my life that my nerves went into a "fight-or-flight" mode and just never returned to normalcy. Because of this, other diseases took hold of my weakened system and had been wreaking havoc on my body all this time. I underwent surgery to remove my gallbladder and ovarian cysts. During my recovery, my fiancé cared for me and kept me comfortable.

We had met just before my work accident at a gas station. He caught me staring at his gorgeous blue paint as he fueled up his old Monte Carlo. We shared a few words and began talking online a few weeks later. His children had been through the same experience I had and he was attempting to recover from his ex-wife's brutal mark on their lives. Just coming out of a bad relationship myself, we decided to go out for drinks a few times. Those drinks turned into dates, and eventually we fell head over heels in love with each other. The children his ex-wife abandoned became my own and I was truly happy.

In the months after my surgery, I recovered and coped with the pain simply by distracting myself. I worked at home, where I was most comfortable editing books and papers. Every time my mind would slip into a dark hole, I would do things that reminded me of how happy I was. I had a cache of pictures of the little family I was a part of, something beautiful I was able to piece back together.

My fiancé bought me a beautiful guitar so I could play whenever I felt lonely or sad. I find, however, that the most effective way to pick up the pieces of a tragedy like mine is to build something beautiful for yourself. It is important to always remember that there are other humans in this world that have suffered the way we have, although sometimes it may be hard to believe. It's important to create strong, unbreakable relationships with people in your life who understand you. Those people will be your stronghold when the worst blows in.

The MOST important aspect of recovering from parental abuse for me was to allow myself to finally forgive them, whether I have a continuing relationship with them or not. Holding onto pain, grief and anger is far more toxic than abuse could ever be because even after the fact, you're only hurting yourself. There is no need to "mend" your parental relationship if it is broken, all you must do is forgive them for yourself.

People in this world who are toxic only wish to spread its acidity, and if you aren't willing to stop that process and allow yourself to overcome its effects, you'll eventually only spread it further. Hang onto things in life that make you happy and don't let them go until you realize that it is pointless to be sad or to carry around your pain. You do not benefit from allowing abuse to hold you back. Instead, allow yourself to be let go, to leave the misery with the ones who inflicted it upon you and open yourself up to the world, which is waiting for you to take advantage of the opportunities it gives to find your calling. If you choose to be truly happy with yourself, nothing can hurt you.

Every once in a while, when a memory comes around to haunt me, I pick up the old guitar and play a Pink Floyd song to myself. I tend to my 86-or-so houseplants, which I keep to remind me that they rely on my existence to care for them. I go outside and watch the birds hop all over the place, eating from my feeders and perching in my apple tree because it reminds me to call my grandfather and thank him, for the billionth time, for having the heart to raise and rehabilitate me.

I go into my children's bedrooms to see the things they color and play with so that I know what kind of surprise to buy them next time I go to the store. I keep myself surrounded by things that make me happy and remind me of the most important things in my life because I choose to. I feel like I've really risen out of the mud and bloomed. It is possible to live a happy, healthy life after enduring parental abuse.

You only need to get started.

~~~~~~~~~~~~~~~~~~~~~~

~~~~~~~~~~~~~~~~~~~~~~

Chapter 5a: Sarah's Toxic Parents Story - Childhood Background

On several occasions as children we had to watch [our dad] scream and swear at my mom. On a few occasions, I can recall him hitting her when he was really upset.

Growing up as a child my sisters and I were under a lot of pressure to be successful. My parents both had very successful careers. It was important to them that we were equally successful in our adult years. We were expected to be great and were constantly being compared to each other. We were evaluated against each other based on how smart, athletic, and pretty we were. They would compare our weight, grades, and really anything else measurable. Once we were older they would compare our ability in sports amongst a variety of other activities.

It is still unclear to me what drove my dad to foster this hyper-competitive family environment. He didn't have parents present in his life himself so that could have played into it, but I will probably never know for sure. My mom, on the other hand, was addicted to pain medication and an alcoholic. I believe this could have played into her compulsions. She was obsessed with her appearance too. She would make frequent comments about her wrinkles, and how pretty she was in her youth. She was, and still is, one of the skinniest women I have ever seen. She is constantly weighing herself and trying new skin creams. My mom definitely put us down to make herself feel better.

My dad, on the other hand, was driven more by his desire to actually have the "perfect" family. He is a very smart man, and he holds himself to an unreasonably high standard. He internalized all of our failures. He also still to this day gets really angry. He might have some form of an anger management problem. He would get uncontrollably angry with my mother. On several occasions as children we had to watch him scream and swear at my mom. On a few occasions I can recall him hitting her when he was really upset.

Chapter 5b: Not So Endearing Nicknames

They would yell at us like a lot of parents do, but they would also swear at us. They would say things like, "I didn't raise a fucking stupid child, did I? Are you fucking stupid?"

When we were little kids we each had a derogatory pet name that our parents called us. Although my name is Sarah, my parents liked to call me "Chubby Chunk". My mom came up with it because it took me a little longer to shed my baby fat. Every time I wanted a second piece of pizza or didn't turn down dessert she would say something like, "Honey, our little Chubby Chuck wants another piece." Or she would say, "Oh Chubby Chunk are you sure you want to eat that?"

My older sister was nicknamed Little Toucan, because she had a rather large nose. I can remember specifically having school pictures, and my sister bringing hers home. My mom said, "Awe Little Toucan, you're so cute, too bad for that big nose." She was so self-conscious of her nose when we were little. She grew her hair out so it was long and would try to use it to cover her face in photos.

One of my little sisters was Cabbage Patch, because my mom said she looked like a cabbage patch doll. She had really large eyes, and a large head when she was a child. She was constantly reminded of her "big head". My dad would call her "Fat Head" sometimes too. If she ever tripped or teetered over they would say, "Poor Fat Head, she can't keep her balance with that big head." Or they would say, "Poor little Cabbage Patch tripped."

My other little sister was Stork Bite. She had a birth mark on her forehead she eventually had surgery to remove. It was right in the middle of her forehead, between her eyes going up to her hairline, and was a light pink color. It was thick at the top and thinned out right between her eyes. My parents constantly reminded her of it by calling her Stork Bite. My mom had her hair styled with bangs. She got a beautiful blue headband for her birthday when she was about eight, and my mom gave it to me because "Stork Bite" was not allowed to wear headbands. I did not want to wear it, but she forced me to wear it to church the next day. She kept talking about how pretty I looked in it right in front of my little sister.

We were constantly pinned against each other in competition. During the average car ride, we would play competitive games. We would play memory games or trivia games. The loser would be ridiculed and called dumb by our parents. They would usually mock us in a "joking" way. They would say things like, "Well, it's a good thing you're pretty." Or, they would be harsher, and say things like, "I didn't raise you to be a stupid child. Why don't you get this? Your sisters get this."

When we would do something wrong and get in trouble my parents had a series of strange punishments. They would yell at us like a lot of parents do, but they would also swear at us. They would say things like, "I didn't raise a fucking stupid child, did I? Are you fucking stupid?" Often times we weren't even entirely sure what we did, especially with my mom. If she had too much to drink her punishments would come out of nowhere, and she would go off on different tangents.

When I was five my sister and I got in trouble. I cannot even remember for what now. My mom as a punishment made me cut my sister's hair. Yelling at me the entire time because it wasn't "good" or "straight". I cried the entire time and kept begging her not to make me do it because I didn't know how. The next day my mom took us to the hair salon to fix it. The hair dresser asked what happened, but she made us lie about it.

They would punish us with missed meals too. We were not given a ton of food as children, just the bare minimum. We were all pretty skinny to begin with, so missing meals was a really big deal to us.

Another weird one was one time as a punishment my mom made my little sister eat an entire sleeve of crackers. The crackers dried her mouth out. She was not allowed to have any water, so it was hard for her to breath.

Our mother was always coming up with new and creative ways to punish us. A lot of the time the punishment did not fit the crime. Our punishments were totally random, we would not have done anything wrong but something would provoke her. She would come up with some strange form of punishment, as if to make herself feel better.

The majority of my childhood my father worked for a Fortune 500 Company, and was relatively high ranking, so he was gone Sunday midday through Friday midday. During the week my mom often neglected her parenting duties for drugs and alcohol, leaving us to fend for ourselves on numerous occasions.

Our mother was always available to critique our physical appearance. She really liked to point out my sister's big nose and my other sister's "ugly" birth mark. Our weight was also constantly being brought up in a negative way, even though we were all a healthy size for our age. My dad would terrorize us on the weekends when he was not too busy ignoring us. He would point out our physical flaws, and hammer us with educational questions, calling us stupid if we could not keep up. So, I mostly tried to steer clear of them, but sometimes it was impossible.

Chapter 5c: Where's Mommy?

"She just got home and she's all out of it. She hit the garage door with the car. What should we do?" Mia asked.

One instance that will always stick out in my mind from my childhood happened before my littlest sister was born. My dad was out of town for business, which was normal, and my mom was watching us. She left us just after lunch and did not get home until sometime in the middle of the night. She said she was just running to the store, but in hindsight she must have gone to the bar or something. Below is what I can remember in detail.

Sarah, Age 6

I wasn't sure how long we had been sitting at the kitchen table. My stomach growled and it hurt really bad. I really wanted food. My throat was very dry too, and I was really thirsty. I thought maybe our mom had forgotten about us.

I found a chair and pushed it over to the kitchen sink. I filled up a cup that I had found in one of the lower cabinets with water from the tap. I knew our mom had told us to stay at the kitchen table but it was dark out and she still wasn't home yet.

Dad was out of town somewhere for business. He was gone most of the time for his new job. I did not know him very well or spend much time with him. I hoped mom would not be mad that I had gotten some water. I climbed down off the chair, careful not to spill the water.

Then, I walked back to the table where my sisters were sitting. "Do you want some water?" I asked, as I reached the cup out towards my older sister Mia.

"No, mom told us to sit here, Sarah, and not to touch anything," Mia replied, swatting the drink away like it was poisoned.

"I know but I was so thirsty. Aren't you thirsty too? Mom left when it was still light out and we had just eaten lunch. Now it's dark out so it must be dinner time," I responded. Of course, Mia was thirsty too but she would never admit it. Mia always did what she was told. If our mom had told her to jump off a bridge she would have done it to please her.

"No, I'm not thirsty. Mom will be back soon," Mia replied stubbornly through her dry, sore throat.

"Okay, well I'm going to give Carol some water. Here Carol drink this, okay?" I held the cup out to Carol. Carol grabbed it desperately.

"Mom said no Carol!" Mia shouted. Carol was only three so she didn't care. She drank a few big gulps of the water. Then, as if in slow motion, the plastic cup slipped from her tiny hands. It bounced back and forth on the ground a few times before settling in a pool of water.

"Look what you've done now! Mom is going to kill us. She is going to know we got up!" Mia shrieked. Technically Mia had not gotten up. Carol had, multiple times, but you really cannot expect a 3-year-old to stay seated for more than a minute.

"No, no it's okay I can fix this," I responded running upstairs to the bathroom. I found a big beach towel and soaked up all of the water. Then I wadded the towel up and hid it on the highest shelf in the bathroom. Hopefully by the time they noticed the towel it would be dry and then my mom would never know how it got there, I thought.

Carol was crying now on the floor. She hadn't been doing a good job of sitting still, anyways. She had mostly been wandering around the house while Mia yelled at her. Carol cried for what seemed like forever, complaining the entire time about how her belly hurt. Finally, she fell asleep on the floor. I found a blanket to throw over her.

It was so dark out, and I could not keep my eyes open. I placed myself close enough to the table to hop back in my seat when I heard my mom get home. Then I drifted off too. I am not sure if Mia ever fell asleep, but I kind of doubt it.

"Mom, mom! Are you okay?" I awoke to Mia's voice. It was starting to get light outside. I thought it must have been the next day, but I was not entirely sure. My mom was slumped over in an armchair in the kitchen. She looked like she was sick or something. That must have been why she didn't get home until after it was so dark out, I thought to myself.

"What happened?" I asked Mia, with a little bit of panic in my voice. Mia was too panicked herself to notice.

"She just got home and she's all out of it. She hit the garage door with the car. What should we do?" Mia asked.

I looked at my mom closely. Her eyes were red, and she was still making some noises and breathing. "Let's get her some blankets so she can sleep. She must be sick," I replied. Mia looked so scared. We wrapped our mom up with blankets and put a pillow in the chair with her. Then we took Carol up to bed.

In hindsight, we would both grow to understand our mom had a problem with alcohol. She typically did a really good job of hiding it from the outside world. Most people would have pegged her as the type to never have a drink or pop a pill. This was the first memorable drunken moment we had witnessed with our mom but by no means would it be the last.

Chapter 5d: Preteen and Teen Years

When [my sister] said that she had simply realized she needed gas and had to take a slight detour, he backhanded her so hard it left a bruise. After watching that I never went off my route.

As we got into the teen years, things got progressively worse. My dad was home practicing law again and later ran for senate. The race for senate was an exceptionally bad time because he was under a lot of stress. He would take out a lot of his frustrations with the race on us and our mom. If we spoke to him and he was working on something he would snap at us. We constantly had to hear about how unsupportive we were.

We were treated like a huge inconvenience, unless we were needed for an appearance of some sort. A lot of the same abuse from childhood still persisted. Our looks and intelligence were constantly compared and questioned.

On the one hand, we did not want to see our sisters hurt. On the other hand, if it was your sister it was not you. So, being compared was a tricky thing. I never wanted to be on the negative side of the comparison, even though I hated seeing my sisters tormented. I would like to say I fed into it less than my other sisters, but I think we all put each other down while trying to gain our parents' approval.

By our preteen years my parents had pretty much made up their minds in regards to who was worth their time and who was not. They had determined my older sister was the super smart ugly one, I was a disappointment in all respects, and the younger two were both promising. I was a complete cast off and typically not even acknowledged. My older sister was complimented on her grades and academics but still belittled for her appearance constantly. My two little sisters were prompted to study and look their best. They were probably verbally attacked less.

My mom would viciously attack each of us for our weight. Reminding us that nobody would want to marry a "fatty". She called my older sister a "fat cow" once in the middle of a store, because she could no longer, at 5' 6", fit into a size 0. She would let the skinnier sisters have dinner but would withhold meals from the larger ones saying that "nothing tastes better than skinny." We would still have to sit at the table with the family and watch as they ate dinner. My mom would talk about the meal and how delicious it was. She would say it was a good thing at least some of her daughters were beautiful. Keep in mind none of us were even remotely overweight. It also varied on who was the "fat" one. Usually it was my older sister, simply because she was older. The expectation that she should be as skinny as our little sisters was not even remotely realistic. We were all called fat at one point or another.

While we each had jobs and worked we were not allowed access to any of our earnings during our preteen and teen years. Not having control over any of our finances helped my parents to maintain their control over us. They also went through our cellphone records weekly, and we were not allowed to have any unapproved phone numbers in our cellphones. This made it virtually impossible to have any friends outside of school. When we were at home our phones stayed locked in a desk drawer in the kitchen. Then we would get them back to take with us before we left for school or an approved activity.

We were only allowed to wear the clothing that they had provided for us. No unapproved clothes were allowed. Not that we had money to buy anything extra with anyways. If we received a present or gift from someone that was clothing, my mom would take it away unless she approved of it. On the few occasions we did get to go to a social activity we had to request permission in advance, and then any money needed for the activity would be withdrawn by either my mom or dad from our savings account and given to us. Our savings accounts were not in our own names, so we were not able to access our funds even if we had wanted to. I had never made a purchase on my own until I was 17 years old.

Dating was completely out of the question. It would not even be considered. We were only allowed to go to after-hours school events if we were involved in the activity. I was actually allowed to go to the school dances, and so could my sisters, because we were each on student counsel and involved in the planning process. We had to take our phone with us and check in regularly, though. We also had to go directly home after and were not allowed to hang out with friends outside of the school.

Dating would have been impossible with the phone monitoring and inability to hangout outside of school. It was constantly stressed that dating was a weakness and waste of time at our age. It was not to be done until after you had succeeded in your career. My dad had a mantra about dating that he would repeat to us frequently. It went like this, "First you go to an ivy league college, then you become successful in your career, then, if you feel you must, find someone more successful and get married." This was beaten into our brains. No other thought process would ever have been accepted or tolerated.

In terms of career path, we were not allowed to stray away from science and math. Law school was okay, but only if you wanted to do private practice. If you wanted to go into politics, then you could work as a lawyer for the state. Medical school or engineering were both fine too. Anything involving the arts was made into a big joke by my parents.

We each had a vehicle to be used for our scheduled activities. Each vehicle had a tracking devise in it that was reviewed regularly. If you deviated from your route at all an interrogation would ensue. I never went off my route, but my older sister did once. My dad attacked her about it, accusing her of taking our families assets for granted. When she said that she had simply realized she needed gas and had to take a slight detour he backhanded her so hard it left a bruise. After watching that I never went off my route.

Chapter 5e: Get a Job Kid

If you abide by the terms in this contract you can stay. If you break any of these terms you will need to find accommodations elsewhere," my father said.

One memory from our preteen years really sticks out to me. By this point in my life, our parents had essentially made up their minds about what we were each destined for. They managed their household to accommodate for their opinion. In my case, they were managing me to keep me from interfering with my other sibling's "development". We were given "plans" in our preteen years to keep us on track.

Sarah, Age 11

"There are two kinds of people in this world. Ordinary people and exceptional people. This family will not tolerate ordinary. Do you understand that?" He looked down at me and I shook my head yes. I got the feeling he was trying to tell me I was ordinary and he did not like it. "I can't hear you," his voice was loud now. He liked to raise his voice to get his point across.

"Yes sir. I understand sir," I replied, not making eye contact. Oops, I thought. He hated it when we did not make eye contact.

"You are close to becoming an adult now. It is important to us that you are successful in your adult life. To achieve this success, you will need to commit to being as excellent as you possibly can be. If not for yourself for the family. If you live here and you aren't succeeding and your sisters see that they will think that is all that's expected of them, as well. I have drafted a contract. If you abide by the terms in this contract you can stay. If you break any of these terms you will need to find accommodations elsewhere," my father said.

My eyes welled with tears as I started reading through the contract. Did he mean stay there, as in live at home, I thought to myself.

This binding agreement is entered into as of February 13th 2005, between household member...
It looked like one of his work documents. I continued reading...
Household member will gain employment by the age of 12 and hold employment until they are no longer in the care of Household supervisor _____
Household member will clock 1000 volunteer hours by the end of middle school _____
Household member will clock 1500 volunteer hours by the end of high school _____
Household member will achieve no less than a 4.0 GPA in middle school _____
Household member will achieve no less than a 4.0 GPA in high school _____
Household member will participate on two athletic sports teams per year _____
Household member will abide by a strict no drugs or alcohol policy

_____

The list went on and on. I noticed there were two copies sitting out. I was glad because I thought this might be something I had to hold on to. There was no way I could memorize the entire thing, I thought.

"Um, what am I supposed to do with this?" I asked. I had never been a part of a contract before.

"It's a contract," He rolled his eyes like I was dumb for not knowing that, "By signing it you have agreed to the terms and stipulations outlined. Then you will abide by it until you are 18 years of age and leave the house," he replied.

My hand shook as I picked up the pen that had been set in front of me. I signed my name to every line. The lines that would be held over my head for years to come. I would come to memorize the contract that I, at one time, had thought would be impossible to memorize. He would quote the lines to me all the time. Whenever I was even borderline going to miss a goal I would hear about it.

"Alright, now let's go over your financial obligations," he paged to the next page of the contract. It outlined what my earnings during my teen years needed to be in order to survive independently at the age of 18. The contract had a detailed savings plan, so that I would have a small nest egg when I was 18 and kicked out of the house. This would come to be one of the most helpful things that had happened to me during my childhood years.

"Now, it's obvious you are not going to amount to much," he said, after we had finished covering my savings plan for years 12 to 18. "So, it will be important that you have saved enough money to become financially independent immediately."

My mom was always telling me I would need to find a rich husband. "Why can I not amount to much?" I questioned, wide-eyed. The second the words whimpered out of my lips I remembered it was not wise to ask questions like this. To my surprise he did not yell or get mad. He just wore his normal vacant look he seemed to reserve for me.

"It's not really your fault. You just inherited the bad genes," he responded.

I looked at him quizzically, unsure of what genes he was talking about. Didn't I have his genes, I thought. I didn't dare question him about it again though. My face must have asked the question for me because I got an answer.

"You did not inherit our natural athleticism, nor did you inherit my intelligence like your sisters did," he stated like it was a fact. "In fact, you inherited dyslexia, which isn't your fault it's on your mom's side. So, it is virtually impossible for you to compete with your sisters. I mean don't get me wrong there have been really successful dyslexics in the past, but they are the exception. You are the norm. You are not special," he said.

I continued to stare at him, my eyes brimmed with more tears. He started to grow agitated, "What are you not getting? Are you really that daft? Each one of you is an investment, in a sense. Sometimes you make an investment and the deal has all of the right ingredients from the get go but then you can start to see signs that it just isn't going to pan out. We call it a dud, and all you can do when you start to smell a dud is create parameters to manage it and then accept you're going to lose your money. Now are we clear?"

I could tell he would keep going until I acknowledged that I was the dud, "Yes sir. I will do my part to manage my shortcomings."

"Okay good. It is important to me that you do not disrupt the household or influence your sisters in anyway," he replied, nodding his head slowly as he talked.

"I won't influence my sisters," I replied holding back tears.

"Okay. Now get out of my sight I have a lot to get done," he replied. I left the room slowly, holding back tears, not wanting to make a scene.

The next day I set to work looking for lawful and gainful employment opportunities. My options were limited as an 11-year-old, but I knew with my birthday a mere two weeks away I needed to act quickly to stay in line with the contract I had signed.

I was able to secure a job as a paper girl, earning a promising $20 a day. It was one of two jobs I was able to find that could legally hire a 12-year-old with a parent's signature. It did the trick.

Chapter 5f: Don't You Nose it's all About Appearance?

"Want my advice?" Dad had asked. Not really, Mia thought, but she knew she was going to get it anyway. "Dump him before he dumps

you. With that Goddamn nose it will never last." She was eight at the time.

The teen years were hard for me, but they were hard for all of us. One specific time will always stick out in my mind because it was the day my older sister changed forever.

Mia, Age 14

They had been fighting about it for an hour in their master sweet. Mia was not sure if they knew she could hear and just didn't care or if they were really that oblivious. In fact, all of the siblings could hear, which was embarrassing enough for Mia. They had been having this conversation for over a year now, ever since she became old enough to get her nose fixed.

They had been having the conversation about her slightly larger than normal nose for years. It was one of the first things she could recall knowing about herself as a child. She knew her nose was too big. It was brought up to her so often how could she have forgotten?

"Don't worry honey we can fix it. You just have to be a little older," our mom would say. Funny she could not recall ever mentioning wanting to fix it. Honestly the whole process seemed really unnecessary and really painful.

Mom would say, "She would be so pretty if not for that nose." Or she would say, "I'm so sorry honey, you know it runs on my side of the family. That big ugly nose of yours." She would say, "It's not enough to just be smart. What's on the outside matters too." She would say these things in front of the whole family on a regular basis.

She knew where they stood on the nose. I, who was closest in age to her, had always assured her it was not bad. "It adds character," I would say. She could not tune out our parents, though. How could she when they were our parents.

She could still remember when she had gotten her first boyfriend. She was in first grade. We were not allowed to have real boyfriends in our teen years. She had not mentioned it to our parents because she knew they would not approve. Carol, our other little sister could not help but spill the beans. Mia should not have told Carol.

"Want my advice?" Dad had asked. Not really, MIa thought, but she knew she was going to get it anyway. "Dump him before he dumps you. With that Goddamn nose it will never last." She was eight at the time. The next day at school, she took his advice.

What seemed like several doctor's appointments came to pass and then she was heading to the final appointment. The appointment that would change her face forever, and her life, as Mom kept reassuring her.

"You want this, right Mia?" the nice doctor asked. Mia stood in the doctor's office with Mom and my sisters. It seemed really crowded in the little room.

"Of course, she does. Look at that thing! It's terrible. How can she be expected to go through life with that on her face? It needs to be taken care of," Mom replied matter of fact. The doctor seemed agitated with our mom but he did not say anything.

I stood next to Mia while she sat on the table. The doctor asked her again, and Mom glared expectantly. Mom's eyes could have burned a hole right through Mia while they waited for her response.

"Yes, let's just get it over with please," Mia replied. Her eyes were brimming with tears that rolled down her nose and cheek when she blinked. I thought she must be kind of embarrassed and maybe even scared.

The medical staff took her for what seemed like forever and when Mia woke up she was really out of it. She still cannot recall the ride home. The recovery process was grueling. One whole week with a big splint right in the middle of her face. Her face was black and blue and swollen. It was uncomfortable to sleep, and it felt weird for a long time after the surgery. Two weeks later she started the last quarter of the school year with her new nose.

Mom told everyone that Mia had had a blocked nasal passageway that required surgery so she could breathe better. All of her friends at church would look at Mia sympathetically. They would reassure our mother that she had done the right thing getting the nasal problem taken care of. They would say they were glad that Mia was feeling better now. Mia was under strict orders to never call it what it was, a nose job. She had to keep up the act. She still mentioned to me, on occasion, about how she missed her old face and its character.

Chapter 5g: To Eat or Not to Eat

"You're a pathetic excuse for an athlete and you're not that sharp either. You would think you would at least know how to starve yourself right. Pathetic..."

Amelia was the youngest of all the sisters, and the most weight obsessed. She counted her calories meticulously. She would stress over the number on the scale, weighing herself every morning and every evening. One day, it took a turn for the worse. I can still remember it like it was yesterday.

Amelia, Age 11

Her alarm read 4:30AM when she awoke. She put on her tennis gear and prepared for training because that's what she did every morning. She would train until 7AM, then go to school until noon. After that, more training until 6PM. Then online classes and then bed. Rinse repeat. She was a top 50 USA tennis player and was on track to go Pro or play for the college of her choice, whatever she wanted to do.

The kids at high school probably thought she was weird, but she did not care. They were not like her. They were not winners. It was like our dad said, "Be exceptional, no less." She was exceptional, she thought. She stepped on the scale. 82 pounds at 5-foot 2-inches. It was not the 82 that bothered her it was what came after. The scale read 82.5 and her heart stopped. She did not understand how she could have possibly gained weight. I walked into the bathroom while Amelia was in the middle of her weigh-in routine. I could tell Amelia was agitated but knew better than to say anything.

She walked into the kitchen ready to leave for the day. "No breakfast today?" Mom asked. Amelia's face reddened.

"What is it?" Dad asked, eyes cold.

She could not lie, what was the point? "I weigh 82.5 pounds this morning," she replied.

"Yep, no breakfast today," he said, "fat athletes don't win competitions, and get Division One offers, do they?"

"No sir, they do not," she replied.

"Alright, off you go. Be exceptional," he said as she walked out the door where her teammate's mom was waiting to pick her up.

Be exceptional she thought at morning practice. Be exceptional she thought as she skipped lunch heading straight to afternoon training.

She woke up in the hospital later that day after passing out. They called it dehydration, and the doctors made her promise to remember to drink lots of water on the court. They kept asking her if she had eaten that day. Our dad and sisters all stood in the room with her. His eyes burned holes in her head. She told the doctor of course she had eaten both breakfast and lunch. Dad drove them home and she could tell he was mad. Everyone was quiet the entire way.

As they walked in the door she turned, "I'm sorry." All of the other sisters bee-lined for their rooms, not wanting to be around for this conversation. That is, apart from myself who hung back, worried.

"You're a pathetic excuse for an athlete and you're not that sharp either. You would think you would at least know how to starve yourself right. Pathetic," he retreated into the west wing, leaving her in the kitchen with me, who was staring at her wide-eyed.

"Amelia, are you okay?" I questioned slowly, reaching out for my sister's tiny arm.

She yanked her arm away. "Of course, I'm okay you piece of lard." She turned and retreated into her room. I did not follow, but it sounded like Amelia may have been doing jumping jacks in her room.

Chapter 5h: Let's Cut to the Chase

"When I'm causing myself pain I don't have to think about how mom and dad hurt my feelings. Okay? Can you get that? Trust me they don't care if I do it, they just don't want anyone else to know…" Carol replied.

One of my sisters struggled with depression while she was in her preteen through early adult years. Our parents would make comments about it sometimes when they were disappointed with her about something. For example, "Why don't you just go ahead and do it already?" It is honestly a miracle she is still alive today. She also is interested in women which was highly frowned upon by my parents growing up. They never directly had a conversation about it, but they seemed to make a lot more homophobic comments when she was around. I think they did that in order to discourage her from ever mentioning it to them, or acting on it.

Carol, Age 13

Carol sat with her arms crossed in front of her, and a vacant look on her face. She always had that same vacant look on her face. She always acted like nothing bothered her or got to her.

"Mrs. Glenn, we asked you in today because one of the girls on the team noticed some marks on Carol's inner leg while they were in the changing room before practice yesterday," Coach Brookes stated. "We just want to know if there is anything we can do to help? I have a counselor I can recommend. The school also offers counseling to its students, so that's an option too." She slid some brochures across the table. The brochures heading read, "Signs and Symptoms of Serious Depression".

My sisters and I sat right outside the door waiting. We all knew how our mom was going to respond to this conversation, and it was not going to be pleasant at all.

"Mrs. Brookes, thank you for your concern but my daughter is perfectly fine. There is a reasonable explanation for how she cut her thigh. Isn't that right, Carol?" her mom stared at her strictly. Carol knew saying anything other than it was an accident was not an option.

She just liked how it felt when she cut herself, what was the big deal, she thought. It made her feel something else other than the constant state of pressure she always felt. What was so wrong about liking that, she thought.

She knew exactly who had ratted her out too. Megan, her teammate. They had been getting closer in a more intimate way, and she must have told Coach Brookes she saw the marks. She felt like she could not trust anyone. Sure, Megan would try to justify telling the coach by saying she "cared". I guess she could not have known the havoc she would be reeking on Carol's life. In all fairness, she had tried to talk to her about it before and Carol had totally blown it off. Megan may not have known where to turn.

"Yup, like I told Mrs. Brookes, my spandex shorts just get a little chaffed sometimes," Carol replied.

"See, exactly like I said a logical explanation," our mom replied.

"Mrs. Glenn, Carol, this isn't something you need to go through alone," Coach Brookes started to say slowly, "I would love to offer my support. Carol we all care very much about you."

Mom's face reddened. Now she was going to explode, all of us girls could tell. "Are you calling my daughter a liar, Coach? Because it sounds to me like you're calling my daughter a liar. She is the best rower on your team, in fact she is one of the best lightweight rowers in the country. Do you want us to go elsewhere? That wouldn't look too good for your job, now would it? Anyways, what 'pervy' teammate of Carol's was staring between her legs? I want them kicked off this team! They obviously have some sort of weird, perverse interest in my daughter. I want to know exactly who it is and I want them gone!" She shouted. The girls all cringed in the hallway.

"Alright, I apologize, Mrs. Glenn. I just wanted you and Carol to both know I am here as a support system for you if you ever need me," Coach Brookes replied. She sounded like she was about to wet her pants. Having your job threatened would do that to you.

Carol watched Mom stand and march out of the room. Carol followed close behind because she took that as her cue to leave too. Her three sisters were sitting just outside the office. Great, she thought, they probably heard everything. They walked outside and piled into the car. They drove home in silence.

When they got home, Carol tried to mention it to Mom, "You aren't planning on mentioning this to Dad, right?" she asked. Uh oh, she had forgotten the cardinal rule. Do not speak unless spoken too. That never ended well in our household.

"If you ever get me dragged into a situation like that again. Ever. I swear to fucking God Carol you won't just be playing dead. You will actually wish you were dead when I'm done with you. Now get out of my face," our mother spat. Mom kept mumbling something about Carol being a worthless piece of shit. All of the girls scattered.

Carol ran to her room and escaped in the only way she knew possible, with a small razor blade. I followed Carol into her room. "What are you doing Carol?" I asked, her eyes welled with tears.

"It feels good Sarah. I'm not going to die I promise. It just feels really good to me," she replied.

"But Carol you don't have to do that. Why don't you give me a hug instead? That will make you feel good," I replied.

"That won't help. When I'm causing myself pain I don't have to think about how mom and dad hurt my feelings. Okay? Can you get that? Trust me they don't care if I do it, they just don't want anyone else to know. It's that stupid Megan that's the problem," Carol replied.

I didn't know what to do, so I said goodnight and retreated to my room.

Chapter 5i: Late Teen to Young Adult Years

"You are not wanted here and you most certainly are not welcome anymore. Now you only have 11 minutes left [to leave] so I would get ready to go," my father's voice cut like a knife.

By the time we each hit our late teens and early adult years, our parents' minds were 100% made up about us. I do not have great insight as to what these years were like for my younger sisters, because I was gone at that point, but for myself personally they were pretty bad.

We constantly were threatened with being kicked out of the house. I went to a high school that had an option for the parent to receive an email for each homework assignment and test grade so they could keep up with their kid's scholastics. This was the worst system for us. My parents would maliciously bring up every assignment, quiz, or test grade that was less than an A. In our late teen years as we got closer and closer to eighteen they would constantly remind us that once we turned eighteen we would have to fend for ourselves. They used it as a method of justification for their obsessively looking into our whereabouts, grades, and really everything.

I think if I had not been kicked out, my parents probably would have continued to monitor my "progress" throughout my college years. My older sister was monitored to some degree and would go home on breaks and stuff. I remember she would check in with them regularly and make goal charts and other strategic planning tools my dad liked to use.

One strange rule that I can remember my older sister having to abide by in college was the no dating policy. They would still check her phone records, even after she started paying for her own plan to see who she was talking to. Dating was still completely out of the question, even though she was supporting herself and living virtually independently of them at school.

It's Time to Go

One of my most memorable experiences was being kicked out of the house. It was very sudden. It was especially hard because of how we spent our teen years. I did not have any friends to turn to. I did not have anyone to go stay at their home, because I had never been allowed to hang out with people outside of school. I was completely on my own.

But you know what?

It ended up being the best thing that had ever happened to me.

Sarah, Age 17

It was the summer before college and I had been invited to hang out with a friend, which seldom happened. It was not for a lack of wanting a social life, it's just when you're busy being perfect that does not leave a ton of time for friends outside of school. Also, my parents super controlling rules did not allow much time for a social life. A girl named Ashley had invited me to a movie that evening and I really wanted to go.

"Mom would it be okay if I go to a movie tonight with Ashley Johnson," I asked, trying to sound calm and cool.

"Ashley Johnson, she's a nice girl. Her dad and yours used to do business together a long time ago. I didn't realize you were friends," my mom responded, looking at me expectantly.

"Well, we aren't really, but she invited me and I just really want to see this movie, and a group of people are going. Ashley said she can pick me up and take me," I responded, crossing my fingers and studying my mom's face.

"What time does it end?" my mom replied. I could tell that she was close to saying yes.

"It should be over around 10:15 I think, so I could be back by 11PM," I replied, feeling hopeful.

I could tell my mom was thinking about it. She was mulling it over, trying to decide if this really simple thing was a big deal or not. "Okay fine," she replied finally.

 Ashley arrived just before 7PM to pick me up. Ashley was polite. She walked up to the door and greeted my parents. She made small talk with them about her parents, how they were doing etc. Ashley even pointed out that it was impressive that my dad was running for senate in this year's election. She told him he definitely had her parents' votes. I could tell my parents liked Ashley. Everything seemed to be going well. I thought to myself, if I had time for friends this would definitely be a friend to have.

We walked out the door and I was surprised to see two boys sitting in the backseat of Ashley's car. I did not want to panic, but I was starting to get a bad feeling.

"I didn't realize we were going with boys," I said.

Ashley laughed and rolled her eyes. We got in the car and she started to drive. "We aren't actually going to a movie Sarah. Oh my gosh, isn't she just the cutest?" Ashley laughed. The boys in the backseat started laughing too.

"Oh, okay, well where are we going?" I asked, "Sorry I don't get out much."

Ashley said something about how somebody's parents were out of town and so they were having a party. I was feeling really uneasy at that point.

"Wow, that sounds like a lot of fun," I said, thinking in my head that it did not sound fun at all. "I really do need to be home on time though. My dad has been really strict on curfew with the whole senate thing. I told them I would be home by 11PM, since I thought we were going to a movie that ended at 10:15PM. You can just drop me off back at home now if that would be easier for you," I yammered.

Ashley made a fake pouting face, "Come on Sarah, I have known you since elementary school. You have never been to a party. Now we are graduated seniors and all headed off to college next year. Everyone likes you, you know? Everyone is always saying they wished you got out more. It will be fun, I promise!"

It was not the "fun" that I was worried about, it was my parents. Normal kids might do stuff like this, I thought to myself, but I was not a normal kid. "No, I really should get home," I replied.

"Sarah, we are almost there. Why don't you just come in for a minute and then at about 10PM I'll take you home. Your parents know my parents and my parents think I'm at a movie. If I bring you home now your parents might call my parents and tell them I'm not actually at a movie," Ashley replied.

I thought about it for a second. I really did not want to get Ashley into trouble. She had been really nice to me and nobody ever invited me to anything. It was really nice of Ashley to try to include me in the first place. "Okay fine," I replied, "But I need to be home by 11PM."

"Yay! Sounds good," Ashley replied, "You know maybe you will actually have some fun for once!" I highly doubted it.

Around 10PM I, who had just been sitting in the bathroom for most of the night, set out to find Ashley. There were a lot of people there. I waded through the crowd and finally saw Ashley across the room. I tried to wave but it was too crowded. It looked like she was playing beer pong. I shifted through the crowd and finally was within Ashley's eyesight. "Sarah!" Ashley yelled. She stumbled towards me throwing her arm over my shoulder. She had a red solo cup in her hand. "Hi Sarah, I missed you where have you been hiding?" She giggled.

"Um, Ashley how much have you had to drink?" I asked feeling super uneasy.

"Oh, not a ton, just maybe 3 or 4," she giggled. I could tell she had definitely had more than 3 or 4 drinks. As someone with an alcoholic for a mom I knew when a drinker was not okay to drive.

"Sarah, I need to go home I don't feel so good," Ashley slurred. Perfect, I thought, because I needed to get home too. Ashley's house was not too far from my own home. I could drive Ashley's car and then walk the rest of the way.

"Okay, Ashley let's get you home," I replied, walking her towards the door. We got outside and were standing outside of Ashley's car. Ashley thumbed through her purse in search of her keys. Finally, she found them.

"I found them!" She exclaimed.

"Great," I replied, "Why don't I drive?" It was clear to me Ashley was in no way capable of driving herself home that evening. I reached out for the keys and Ashley yanked them back. She became really mad suddenly. I had seen this kind of behavior before with my mother.

"No!" Ashley yelled. "I can drive myself," she stomped her foot and headed for the driver's side door.

"Ashley, I really don't think that's a good idea," I started to say but Ashley was too quick. She slammed the door and took off, swerving down the drive.

Oh God, I thought, that was my only ride. Everyone else inside was drinking a ton and most of them were just staying the night. Not that I would have felt comfortable asking anyone else for a ride but desperate times called for desperate measures.

It was now 10:30PM and I really needed to get home. I pulled out my flip phone and tried calling Mia. No answer. She was probably asleep. I walked back inside finally, "Excuse me do you have the number of a cab company?" I started asking around the room. "Excuse me are any of you driving home?" No sober takers on that one.

Finally, I found someone with a cab company's number. I opened my wallet which had $15 cash, enough for a movie ticket and a snack. I dialed the cab company. "Hi um I need a cab. How much would it be from Hoover Avenue to Jameson Court?" I asked.

They told me it would be $50. "Oh, okay, I only have $15 on hand but when I got home I could probably get about $20 more from my sister," I heard a click. "Hello?" "Hello?" They had hung up and it was now 11PM.

It had to have been a ten mile walk home. By the time I made it, it was at least 2AM. My feet were sore, and my mouth was dry with thirst. I was soaked because it had started raining about half way through my walk. It definitely had not been a safe walk home, but I really needed to get back so I did not get in trouble.

I crept up to my room, and then woke up at 6AM the next morning. I walked downstairs ready to explain what had happened to my parents and apologize profusely. When I reached the bottom of the stairs I saw two suitcases packed neatly next to the table. Both of my parents were standing there. A sinking feeling set in. "Please let me explain," I started.

"There is nothing to explain," my dad replied. "You have violated the terms of our agreement. We have packed what you own and you can have 15 minutes to get changed and grab whatever sentimental items you think you can carry."

"No please, I swear I never meant to be late, please don't do this I don't have anywhere to go," I replied. I could hear my sisters and knew they were in the room next door listening but pretending not to.

"I have withdrawn $100 from your bank account and put it solely in your name. Here is the information. This debit card links to your account. It is everything you've earned since living here." he handed me a piece of paper with some numbers on it and a card. I had never had access to my own money before. I had never been allowed to buy anything. I was just supplied with clothes and food by my parents.

"Please I don't know where to go," I tried again.

"Stop Sarah. Just stop. You know, three out of four kids with the potential to be exceptional isn't bad, but you are bringing the rest of us down and I simply can't have that. You are not wanted here and you most certainly are not welcome anymore. Now you only have 11 minutes left so I would get ready to go," his voice cut like a knife.

I turned around and walked upstairs to my room. I looked around at my childhood room. I walked over and opened my drawer, realizing they had already emptied them. That must have been what the suitcases were full of. There was a single outfit that had been laid out on a chair for me. I put it on. Jeans, a white V-neck, and tennis shoes. When had they had time to do this, I thought. While I slept?

That was so creepy. I scanned the room one last time and realized I did not own anything of sentimental value. I walked downstairs still with two minutes to spare. I grabbed a suitcase in each hand and walked out the door. I was not sure, but I thought I heard one of my sisters crying quietly.

I did not have anywhere to go, but I did have enough money for a cab now. I called the cab company, whose number I still had from the night before, and in 20 minutes they were there to pick me up.

"Where you headed?" the cab driver asked.

"Bus station," I replied. We drove in silence. I got to the bus station and a small part of me hoped I would get a call asking me to come back. I knew that call was not coming, though.

"Where are you headed?" The lady behind the window asked. Crap, I thought, I was not sure. I looked at the out-bound board. There were so many possible choices. "Honey, where are you headed?" the lady asked again.

"Chicago, I'm headed to Chicago," I replied with a definite tone.

Chapter 5j: Today

We all have gone in our own directions now. I am blessed to still get to speak to all of my sisters, however, that is not the case with everyone in my family. I have been able to work towards healing and have a really great support system at home.

I think for the most part we are all in a better place. I do not think any of us, apart from Mia, will ever be particularly close with our parents. Even though I do not wish them any ill, I do not want them to be a close part of my life, either.

Sarah, 29

It's many years later and I have a family of my own. I have two beautiful children and a loving husband. I graduated with honors from a state school. I have a great career in sales and marketing. I started therapy when I was 17 and never stopped going. I lived in Chicago for a while but have since moved a number of times. After my strict, non-social upbringing I love traveling to new places and meeting new people. I still have to work constantly to live above my upbringing, but with the help of my husband and therapist I have been able to overcome a lot of my obstacles.

One of the main things I still struggle with is self-image. Constantly wanting to look perfect and worrying too much about the number on the scale is still an obstacle for me. I can still hear my mom's voice sometimes in the back of my mind telling me to put makeup on, straighten my hair, or paint my nails.

Trust is another big area I struggle with. It is hard for me to trust that anyone will love me unconditionally without strings attached. That is another area that therapy has really helped me to overcome.

Believe it or not, I actually do talk to my parents occasionally. They reached out after 5 years when I was about to get married. They strongly pushed to be involved with my children but they are not allowed.

Mia, 31

Mia is a lawyer. She graduated from an ivy league school before going on to pursue her legal degree. She does not have a family of her own and often says she has no desire to ever have one. She, like our father, is pursuing a career in politics. She has not received any therapy as of this writing and has no desire to. She still talks to our mom and dad on a regular basis. To my knowledge she abuses alcohol regularly and takes pills to cope, similar to my mother. The last time I spoke to her I tried to convince her to seek help, but she is really not interested.

Carol, 27

Carol went to an ivy league, division one school for rowing. She attempted to kill herself during her junior year because she was not offered the number one spot on the team. After her failed suicide attempt her school was able to get her involved with their counseling program. After receiving counseling for a number of years she cut off all communication with everyone in our family apart from me.

She now lives happily in the Pacific Northwest with her girlfriend. They are both attending law school. She wants to work for her state in public prosecution and put the bad guys away. She is particularly interested in prosecuting domestic violence cases. Her girlfriend is studying to become an environmental lawyer. Carol plans on proposing next year when they graduate. She wants to have children of her own someday but recognizes she may need therapy to help her be the best parent she can be.

Amelia, 24

Amelia is currently in medical school. She graduated college after playing division one tennis at a state university. She is receiving therapy for an eating disorder now. She was hospitalized after her eating disorder became so severe in college that it almost took her life.

She now acts as an advocate for women with eating disorders and leads a support group. She has no communication with our parents but still speaks to Mia and myself. She wishes Carol would reach out but realizes she probably will not do so any time soon. They had a particularly rocky time after Mia and I had both left the house, constantly being pinned against each other.

Chapter 5k: Advice to the Reader

Never give up on being the person you want to be, because being a kind, considerate, good person is what is truly exceptional.

If you are struggling or have struggled in the past with a verbally abusive home life I would encourage you to seek help. Counseling has been instrumental in bettering my mental state. It is important to work with a counselor who fits your personality. If you go to a few different people and it takes a bit of time to find the right fit don't stress about that. I saw several therapists before finding the right fit for me.

My next piece of advice is find your support system. Whether that is your significant other or friends it is important to have people you can talk to. I have found great comfort in my support system of close friends and loving husband. One of my little sisters is very involved with her support group for individuals who suffer from eating disorders, and that has been immensely helpful for her. Knowing you have people who love you unconditionally and are there for you can really help.

Lastly, forgive and move forward. I think it is important to understand the fine line between forgiving and forgetting. Forgiving is something you do for yourself, not for them. I have forgiven my parents, even though they have not asked for my forgiveness, because forgiveness is necessary for a settled spirit. Having non-forgiveness or hate in your heart does you more harm over the course of your life than it will ever do to them. However, I will never forget how I was treated, so as to not make the same mistakes with my children, nor will I ever allow my parents to treat my kids negatively.

You have to move forward with your life. Every day I work on being a better person than I was the day before. I am by no means perfect. It's a rarity but sometimes I have a bad day and snap at my husband for silly little things like not taking the garbage out. It's like hearing my mom, but then I realize it was my own voice and I just snapped. When that happens, it feels terrible but you have to pick yourself up, apologize, and then keep working towards being your best self.

Never give up on being the person you want to be, because being a kind, considerate, good person is what is truly exceptional.

~~~~~~~~~~~~~~~~~~~~~~~~~~~~~~~~~~~~~

Note from the authors and publisher: Did you find this book interesting and helpful? Would you do us an enormous favor and review the book so that others may see that it could be of help to them, as well?

Thank you!